IN ALL THINGS

God's Providence

To Mary,

from Chuck & Mary

1 Peter 5:7

DR. JOHN NEUFELD

Tellwell Talent
www.tellwell.ca

ISBN
978-1-998048-00-7 (Hardcover)
978-1-998048-02-1 (Paperback)
978-1-998048-01-4 (eBook)

TABLE OF CONTENTS

INTRODUCTION

What's Behind Our Experiences?

The flip of a coin

We humans not only experience life, but seek meaning in it. We are destined, by virtue of having been created in the image of God, to make sense of what we experience. It's never enough to say something simply happened, we want to know how and why, and also whether it is good or bad, right or wrong. We constantly decide whether we will dismiss an event or make much of it. We evaluate, judge and seek to understand our experiences.

Here's an easy example of this: you turn on your television set, preparing to settle into several hours of watching a football game. The first event that occurs is the coin flip to determine how the game will begin. Will the winner of the toss receive the ball, or will they decide to kick it away to the other team? After one team wins the coin toss, most of us quickly forget about this act as a matter of small significance that is unlikely to determine the outcome of the game. The game will be decided by a number of more significant factors. We conclude that even if the coin toss provided one team with an advantage, it was a slight one.

But consider another example. A windstorm knocks over a large oak tree. It smashes onto a house, destroying half of it. The house is occupied by a young couple who had moved in the day before. They noticed the house had two identical bedrooms on opposite sides of the house. The day they moved in they couldn't decide which bedroom to sleep in, so she said, "Let's flip a coin! Heads we take the southside room, tails we take the northside." And they abide by the coin. That night, the tree destroys the bedroom they did *not* choose, saving them from certain death. In this case, their brush with disaster caused them to spend a great deal of time wondering about the seemingly minor coin toss. They did not dismiss it as a matter of small significance, as they would have when watching the football game; indeed, their lives were saved due to this seemingly random event.

The coin toss itself was a simple act, a matter of little significance. Who has not flipped a coin? But it was the events that transpired after it that were of great significance. A coin toss is simply a physical action governed by the law of averages. There was a 50 percent chance that the coin toss would come out heads, and a 50 percent chance it would not. In the first example, it didn't really matter which way the coin fell; in the second it did. Had the coin fallen differently, the young couple would have perished.

Is anyone in charge of a coin toss?

After their near-death experience, the couple began processing their experience, wondering, *What happened when that coin was flipped? Was the outcome just a matter of dumb luck?* They might write off what happened as being part of the laws of probabilities, the idea that events can be predicted based on frequency of occurrence and repetition. But further reflection made them conclude there was more at work than a random turn of events. *Why did we decide to flip a coin? Why did we assign the south bedroom to tails? Clearly there is more here than the flip of the coin. Did God direct the coin so we would live? Would the same also be said if the tree had fallen on our bedroom and we had perished? Does God direct both good fortune and disaster?*

It is not possible to experience the world without wondering about it. But the conclusions we come to are varied. The ancient Greeks and Romans believed the gods were fickle and unpredictable and could punish humanity on a whim. Could they have been right? Some faiths believe we are governed by karma and will be made to repeat lessons from failures in past lives. Is this true? Others believe in a spiritual law of sowing and reaping. Perhaps our couple had done good things in the past, and they reaped the results. Is this spiritual law as powerful as the law of probability? It's certainly lauded in popular culture. For example, in the old movie *The Sound of Music*, Maria believes that meeting Baron von Trapp was a reward for something good she did in the past. She believes the amazing change in her circumstances came about because her good deeds triggered forces for good. Should the couple who flipped the coin think the same? Were they reaping what they had previously sown?

What is the nature of our experiences? And how do we interpret them? Are our experiences governed by pure luck, laws of nature, fate, or unseen spiritual forces? Did the outcome of the coin toss come about because of good things done in the past? How should our couple explain their experiences?

The idea of providence: What if God oversees all things?

Who among us has not asked, "Why did this happen to me?" in either gratitude or despair. Who among even the most abject agnostics has not asked God for help at one time or another? Why ask for divine help if we are convinced none is forthcoming? This book is about providence, more specifically the doctrine of the Providence of God, which is tied to His sovereignty and is taught throughout scripture. The doctrine of Providence is an invitation to reinterpret virtually everything we experience. To put it another way, if one accepts the doctrine of Providence, one will see the hand of God in each moment and in every circumstance and will never experience life the same way again. Indeed, God will never seem far away again.

For many people, including some Christians, the doctrine of theistic naturalism is the solution. Naturalism is the belief that nature is all that exists. For this reason, all naturalists are atheists. But *theistic* naturalists are a sort of hybrid. On one hand, they believe God *does* exist, and that the world we live in is the product of His intelligent design, and on the other they believe the world is inconsistent with God and that nature and God have separate, even competing, spheres of sovereignty.

Theistic naturalist beliefs go something like this: God created the world and is looking out for it. But human beings fell from grace, resulting in a cursed creation. God continues to oversee and care for this flawed world, especially human beings who, while sinners, are the crown of His creation. Further, He is in charge and moving all history and humans toward their final goal: the return of Christ. When Christ returns the curse on creation will be removed, but in the meantime things are not as they should be. In this world we experience blessings with bounty and threats of disaster in the form of disease, hurricanes, earthquakes and physical suffering. In this world, one flip of the coin can change everything.

Is this true? Is God little more than the world's designer? Most people of faith, and certainly most Christians, would reject this; even theistic naturalists believe God intervenes in the form of miracles. But sometimes, for mysterious reasons, God chooses *not* to intervene, allowing suffering, misery and evil to carry on without intervention. Why? Theistic naturalists believe God has wise and glorious reasons for not intervening, and that if nature sometimes allows trees to fall on houses, crushing the occupants, it's not the work of God. "That's a fallen creation!" they say. "It's nature expressing sovereignty within its sphere of authority." And to theistic naturalists, that explains everything from war to cancer, and they believe this duality will continue until Christ returns and brings all things under His rule.

This perspective claims to be hopeful in that it holds that all things will eventually work out to God's glory and the world's good. But it also holds that in the meantime nature will function *only* according to the laws of nature, which has ramifications. Tectonic plates shift. Earthquakes ensue. Houses collapse. People are killed. Cells mutate. Cancers form and grow. Children sometimes die. Parents weep. In a fallen world, people act out of sinful and unrighteous motives. Power groups form. Nations go to war. Heinous acts occur. Innocents are killed. Families suffer. All these events, according to theistic naturalists, occur because of dualism of God and nature.

Strangely, many Christians assume this is the Christian worldview and have never heard of other options. And yet, some of the great statements of faith in the Protestant world deny this viewpoint. The Westminster Confession of Faith, Chapter V, says:

God, the Great Creator of all things, doth uphold, direct dispose, and govern all creatures, actions, and things, from the greatest even to the least, by His most wise and holy providence, according to His infallible foreknowledge, and the free and immutable counsel of His own will.

According to this, there is *not one event* that is not directed by God. Let me say it again: not one event! Not one large event, not one small! All are governed by God.

The Heidelberg Catechism is even more explicit: "What do you understand by the providence of God?" it asks. The recitational reply is:

God's Providence is his almighty and ever-present power, whereby, as with his hand, he still upholds heaven and earth and all creatures, and so governs them that leaf and blade, rain and drought, fruitful and barren years, food and drink, health and sickness, riches and poverty, indeed, all things, come to us not by chance, but by his fatherly hand.

So, what is true? Contrary to theistic naturalism is the belief of God's absolute and meticulous sovereignty, the view that God is a grand micromanager who is actively involved in all things and that there is no event God does not control.

What does the Bible teach?

Let's consider some scriptures that speak to this. Psalm 104 (a Creation psalm) speaks to God's glorious creation of water, clouds, mountains and streams. It mentions grass for livestock, food for the beasts of the forest, plants for humans to eat and the moon that marks the seasons, among other things. According to Psalm 104, verses 27–30 (ESV):

These all look to you, to give them their food in due season. When you give it to them, they gather it up; when you open your hand, they are filled with good things. When you hide your face, they are dismayed; when you take away their breath, they die and return to their dust. When you send forth your Spirit, they are created, and you renew the face of the ground.

Psalm 104 doesn't tell us that the physical laws govern the property of all things, but that the open hand of God causes all of nature to flourish at each moment, and His hidden face causes nature to wither and die.

The same thought is expressed in Psalm 135:6–7:

Whatever the Lord pleases, He does, in Heaven and on earth, in the seas and all deeps. He it is who makes the clouds rise at the end of the earth, who makes lightnings for the rain and brings forth the wind from His storehouses.

So according to these Psalms, God is *not* restricted by the forces of nature, and nature does not act on its own. When there is lightning, wind or rain, it is because He has brought it out of His storehouse on that day, and this is also true when there is sunshine. In fact, it applies to all laws of nature. Jesus thought this way. Notice his affirmation of God's sovereignty over all events in nature.

Are not two sparrows sold for a penny? And not one of them will fall to the ground apart from your Father [Matthew 10:29].

This illustrates divine Providence, which invites us to see God in ordinary events, not just in extraordinary ones. Divine Providence holds that God is sovereign over all things, and study of this belief becomes an invitation to encounter God as never before and to reconsider every experience one has had or will have.

The great English preacher Charles Spurgeon once gave a sermon based on Ezekiel 1:15–19, in which he asserted that God's control over creation was complete. It is God who moves the planets and galaxies, the dust particles in a sunbeam, the spray of droplets against the bow of a boat, the descent of leaves in autumn and the tumbling of an avalanche.[1] Indeed, Spurgeon was right. The universe is, in every place, charged with the grandeur of God. You and I have never experienced a moment when God was not directing all things. We have never been out of his presence. He has never been silent. He has never *not* been sovereign.

---

[1]   Spurgeon, Charles. "God's Providence," sermon on Ezekiel 1:15-19, Bible Bulletin Board.

CHAPTER 1

What Does Providence Mean?

God directs the properties of all things in the universe to act precisely as they do. God fulfills His purposes in all things. The earth is the Lord's. He created all of it to display His glory. He governs the ongoing properties of all things for the same reason. And that is Providence. By "Providence," we mean God governs all things for His glory and the eternal good of the people He has chosen by His grace.

There is of course a secular definition of the word "providence." Sometimes we hear people say that everything happens for a reason. They may or may not mean that God directs all things. For some, the reason behind all things remains a mystery that can't be understood. But that doesn't mean that some force is not guiding matters. For instance, imagine that a person has a setback in life, only to discover it opened up possibilities that would not have been there had the setback not occurred. They think about what has transpired and say that "all things happen for a reason." There is no confidence in that statement that God governs all things for His glory and for the good of the people He has chosen. Nor is there a sense that the good that has occurred came about because of the mercy of God on the undeserving. Instead, they simply believe that there is purpose rather than random events.

But the biblical view of Providence confidently sees it as always originating from God. God directs all things for His glory!

An alternative Christian view (practical deism)

Many Christians, failing to grasp what the Bible describes, hold a contrary view. They are practical deists. Deism was a popular worldview both in the 1600s and 1700s. Deists taught that God was much like a watchmaker. Like a watch with springs and wheels, deists imagined that God wound up the world, allowing it to wind down in the way he had designed it to operate. He does not intervene in his creation; he designed it to act on its own.

Deists did believe in a creator. Furthermore, they believed that the universe reflected His glory. But they denied that the creator was actively involved in his creation. The deists believed that God created the laws of physics and the incredible complexity of all things. But once having created it, God went away. Some thought that to enter his creation was a sign the creator was not satisfied with his work. Like a poor watch or a badly designed car, a bad creator would constantly need to fix that which had not been designed well. Looking for God is like looking for an imperfect deity. Others argued that God either became bored with his work or had gone on to complete other projects. God was no longer present to his creation.

Christians are not deists, hence there can be no consistent form of Christian deism. Sadly, a great many Christians today appear to be either partial or practical deists. I mean that theologically; they do believe that God controls all things. But practically they don't live in that reality. When unexpected coincidences or bad things happen, like the loss of health or jobs or the breakdown of relationships, they do not see the hand of God. When an earthquake shakes the ground or a volcano erupts, they think of it in terms of chance or physical mechanisms. "That's just how a broken and fallen universe works," they say. "We had the misfortune of being caught up in the principles of the outworking of nature."

How sad! Rather than seeing God's hand in all things, they assume many things have nothing to do with God at all. Furthermore, many have never been taught either the doctrine of God's Providence or how to translate that doctrine into moment-by-moment trust in God. What is lacking is a rigorous examination of what the Bible actually claims about the works of God.

What does God's providence mean for miracles?

Part of the confusion about Providence is related to an understanding of miracles. For some, a miracle is an indication that God has become involved. The lack of a miracle is an indication that God simply allowed things to carry on. For our purposes, we need an answer to a fundamental question: what's the difference between Providence and miracles? I am arguing that God is always intervening in all things. God no more intervenes in a miracle than he does in the regular daily events of life. But if that is so, what is a miracle, if not direct divine intervention?

Consider C. S. Lewis's important book on miracles.[2] When explaining a miracle, Lewis gives an illustration. Imagine a pool table that has a perfectly level and predictable surface, excellent cushions and so forth, that allows for predictable outcomes. When the pool player banks a ball off the cushion and into the side pocket, it is the rules of physics that determine if the ball will go in. If the pool shot is made with skill, with the proper angle considered, the ball will go into the pocket on every occasion. No miracle has occurred. What happened was governed by the laws of nature.

But what if, while making the shot, someone reaches down onto the table and catches the ball in his hand? He then puts the ball not into the side pocket, but into his own pants pocket. The natural order of events has been interrupted by a hand reaching down from outside of the table.

And that, argues Lewis, is the definition of a miracle. God is supernatural. This means he is not to be identified with the creation or the natural laws which govern it. Rather, he is the creator, whose existence is apart from the natural order. Given that reality, Lewis then argues that a miracle occurs when God interrupts the course of nature by reaching his hand into the creation. The expected outcome is overridden because of his intervention. This is what occurred when the Red Sea parted and when the leper was instantly cleansed. The normal guiding hand of nature was interrupted by the intervention of God.

That sounds like an attractive definition of a miracle. When I was a young Christian, that's the viewpoint that attracted me. Whether it was the incarnation or Joshua's sun standing still in the sky, I wanted to

---

[2]   Lewis, C. S. *Miracles*. London: Collins, 2012.

tell people that sometimes God interrupts the laws of nature he put into place. He enters his creation by suspending natural, observable laws. Furthermore, he does so to declare his presence as well as to display his mercy.

But as I matured and studied my Bible, I began to doubt that this was really a biblical definition of a miracle at all. It was my study of Hebrews 1:3 that really caused me to question Dr. Lewis's definition. I became fascinated with the idea that at each moment, not just occasionally, God was sustaining the universe. God does not occasionally reach his hand into the pool table, but his hand is *always* in the pool table. The pool table has never known a microsecond when his hand was not there.

Consider Colossians 1:15–16:

> He is the image of the invisible God, the firstborn of all creation. For by him all things were created, in heaven and on earth, visible and invisible, whether thrones or dominions or rulers or authorities—all things were created through him and for him.

Colossians indicates not just that God created all things, but that all things serve his purposes. This in itself is a breathtaking claim. This means that all events, including those that occur in the invisible and the visible realm, are occurring to proclaim his greatness. Or to put it into the negative, nothing that occurs deters from the honor that is rightly due to God.

Then comes the next verse, Colossians 1:17: "And he is before all things, and in him all things hold together."

To say that all things hold together in him is to say that Jesus, the Son of God, the great uncreated Creator, is at all moments causing things to exist. We must conclude then that there are no rogue atoms or rogue events. All that occurs is directed by his hand.

But if that is so, what is a miracle? For indeed, the Bible does record them. When miracles occur, it seems like the laws of nature have been suspended, just as Dr. Lewis said. But if God is sustaining all things at each moment, how can there be a difference between a miracle and any regular daily occurrence?

Consider Luke 7:11–17:

> Soon afterward he went to a town called Nain, and his
> disciples and a great crowd went with him. As he drew
> near to the gate of the town, behold, a man who had
> died was being carried out, the only son of his mother,
> and she was a widow, and a considerable crowd from
> the town was with her. And when the Lord saw her, he
> had compassion on her and said to her, "Do not weep."
> Then he came up and touched the bier, and the bearers
> stood still. And he said, "Young man, I say to you, arise."
> And the dead man sat up and began to speak, and Jesus
> gave him to his mother. Fear seized them all, and they
> glorified God, saying, "A great prophet has arisen
> among us!" and "God has visited his people!" And this
> report about him spread through the whole of Judea and
> all the surrounding country.

From the observable laws of nature, what should have happened?
When this young man died, his heart stopped beating and his blood
pooled. Then his body changed colour and became cold. With that his
body began to break down. Proteins started to decompose. The cell
walls broke down and there was a loss of cohesion between tissues,
resulting in the liquefaction of all his internal organs. All of this was to
be expected. All of this was a part of the regular processes we observe
in nature.

But something different occurred. Jesus commanded this
decomposing process to cease. At His word the decay immediately
reversed itself. The heart began to beat and the blood rushed life to
organs that were immediately repaired. It is remarkable! Such things
are not expected. They belie what we know of nature.

Was it that God, reaching His hand onto the pool table, interrupted
the natural course of nature? I am arguing this is not what we are
observing. I have said the normal course of nature is no more than Jesus,
the great Creator, constantly directing the course of all things. And if

this is so, it is no more remarkable that the dead should rise than that the sun should rise each morning.

What then is a miracle? From my perspective, **a miracle occurs when God sustains all things in an extraordinary manner.** Instead of intervening in predictable patterns, he chooses to intervene in an unpredictable pattern. We witness God acting in ways that are not typical of His normal designs.

And if we had eyes to see it, we would come to the correct conclusion: God's hand is never far off. Indeed, his hand is always present. That's why Paul would say, "In him we live, and move and have our being" (Acts 17:8).

We conclude then that God is always acting in nature. He is always intervening in the realm of the visible and the invisible. He is always sustaining all things. When a miracle occurs, God is acting outside of His predictable norm. That's the difference between God's providential rule and His miraculous deeds. But make no mistake, nothing has changed. God is never not active. The universe doesn't run itself.

Every one of us experiences remarkable events during our earthly lives. Those who do not believe in a guiding, superintending hand overseeing all things may call these events "coincidences" and think of them as random happenstance. Or they may view them from the perspective of spiritual forces either rewarding or punishing them, or even that the gods are fickle.

But as we have mentioned before, there is a biblical alternative to this view of the world. It is the view that God directs the properties of all things in the universe so that they act precisely as they do. God fulfills His purposes in all things. The earth is the Lord's. He created all that is for His glory. He governs the ongoing properties of all things for His glory. Furthermore, God governs all things for the eternal good of the people He has chosen by grace. This view of things is called Providence.

In the news

At one time in my life, while I served as a pastor of a large and influential church in my community, my name came up in the news. I first heard my name on the radio while driving into church and knew that something had occurred. I was being charged with giving leadership to a protest against a school board program combatting homophobia. Furthermore, a newspaper reporter who was covering a community protest about the school program wrote an article about me portraying me as homophobic.

What had happened was that some members of my church, concerned about religious denigration inherent in the program, had joined a community protest seeking balance. The reporter realized that some of my church's congregation were among the protesters, and without checking the veracity of the claims she was making or contacting me, wrote about my presumed involvement in attempting to silence the voices of marginalized people.

I had made no statements about the new school program. For one, I had not read the actual proposal for the schools. Like many, I had heard about it and was concerned. But up to then I had said nothing. I was not yet in a place where I could offer an educated and helpful comment. However, some parents, realizing the program for what it was, formed a protest. Some of them had mentioned the name of the church they attended.

Let me be clear. When this reporter wrote a thorough denunciation of me, she did so without interviewing me, or other leaders in our church. Like so much of contemporary news reporting, facts are often lost in favour of the controversy a story will create. Controversy creates interest. The fact that I was a mega-church pastor surely didn't help my cause. The conclusions were reached before I had spoken. In short, the article was partly factual. Yes, some members of my church were protesting. Yes, some members had drawn attention to the church they attended. But they never said that the protest was organized by the church, nor that the leadership of their church was aware of it. But that didn't matter. The story took shape and a narrative was created.

I wondered how to respond. Of course I wanted to say that I held to the historic Christian positions on sex and sexuality. We were, after all, a biblically centered church. But how we respond to a secular community is another matter. An old friend was then in town, and we had coffee together. He directs a missions agency in Europe and is only occasionally in North America. During our conversation I told him about the reporter and the malicious article. We prayed and he gave me valuable counsel about how to respond with grace.

Seated by God

Shortly after that my friend returned to Europe. Seated next to him on the plane was a woman and, as often happens on long flights, the two engaged in conversation. He soon realized that the woman was the very reporter who had written the article about me and my church. This gave my friend the opportunity to not just defend me, but to explain what my church was all about. He told of the multicultural services we had, and of the work that had been done by the church. The reporter marvelled that she had in fact not known anything about the church.

Was this unplanned meeting the result of an incredibly unlikely coincidence? Or was it divine Providence? Two individuals on the same flight with randomly assigned seats, seated next to each other for hours. With all the flights they could have chosen, all the days they could have travelled and all the seats available on that flight, these two were seated next to each other. My friend was given the opportunity to explain not just my church, but the Gospel that was being preached. Was this a coincidence? Or is every encounter we experience directed by the hand of God? Should we be surprised that such things happen?

Scripture is clear that all is ordered by His divine will. God constantly maintains and watches over everything He has made. He consistently and continually directs His creation, causing each thing to act the way that it does.

What else does the Bible say about Providence?

Jesus was much more than a great prophet, teacher and miracle worker: "He is the radiance of the glory of God and the exact imprint of His nature, and He upholds the universe by the word of His power" (Hebrews 1:3).

Jesus is not the reflection of God, He is the actual *radiance* of God. Think of it this way. The light we see from the moon is reflected. The light we see from the sun is the radiance itself. The Bible does not teach that Jesus reflects the glory of the Father, but that he is the very glory itself. Furthermore, the one who is the very essence of glory is also the one who sustains, or upholds, the universe. This means that Jesus is constantly caring for all aspects of it and ensuring that, moment by moment, all things are accomplishing the purposes for which He made them. How does He do it? By His powerful word. When Christ, the ruler of the universe, utters a command, the universe obeys.

An obvious example of His power is found in the story of the loaves and fish. It is recounted in Matthew 14:13–21, and says Jesus took five loaves of bread and two fish and started breaking them so he could feed 5,000 people. In His hands the molecular structure of bread and fish were multiplied exponentially, because He is master of all that exists.

In verses 22–33 of that same chapter, Jesus walked on water. How is that possible? And yet He did it. His body continued to be fully human, subject to natural forces, and so the implication seems to be that He changed the composition of the water below His feet as He walked by controlling its molecules at each microsecond of time.

Think about that: at each moment, the structure of all created things, including human beings, is subject to His will. According to the writer of Hebrews, Jesus directs the physical universe to act precisely as it does—He upholds the universe. Earth remains on its axis, rotating around the sun at precisely the speed it does, because Christ dictates at each moment that it should do so.

Psalm 103, written by the most godly king of ancient Israel, King David, is a song of wonderful praise and thanksgiving to God for this immense care He takes of His creation. Verse 1 begins with the familiar words "Bless the LORD, O my soul, and all that is within me, bless His holy name!"

Verses 3–5 provide reasons to bless God:

> Who forgives all your iniquity, who heals all your diseases, who redeems your life from the pit, who crowns you with steadfast love and mercy, who satisfies you with good so that your youth is renewed like the eagle's.

Many of us have been struck by the poetic nature of these words. They acknowledge God's promise to do good for His people, but they also acknowledge God's high level of control in day-to-day affairs. God controls forgiveness from iniquity (sin or evil). God controls whether one recovers from or succumbs to illness. God controls whether one overcomes obstacles or sinks into a pit of despair (or the pit of hell). God controls the beauty and joy one experiences in life. God controls vitality as you age.

All these things speak to specifics. Details. Big and little things. This is what is meant by Providence. God doesn't just *occasionally* intervene, he *always* intervenes. God's Providence finds its way into every aspect of our lives.

God's hand in everything

When we Christians say God is in control, or that He is sovereign, what exactly are we talking about? Does He control the major events of life but leave lesser matters to us? If we lose our jobs, is God directing that? How about if we lose our car keys, credit cards or favourite ball cap? Is there a difference between our negligence and God's control? Or does God control our negligence? Is God directing us when we drive over the speed limit and get a ticket? Or, far more seriously, is God directing us when we hit a patch of ice and crash the car, when we are diagnosed with cancer or when our spouses tell us they no longer love us? What does God's meticulous sovereignty mean, anyway, in reality?

How can a sovereign God allow war? Why would God willfully allow an unethical employee to steal your company's much-needed funds? What about kidnapping, assault, rape and the host of societal evils we are appalled by? Does He control our free will to make moral choices? If so, do we even *have* free will?

These are questions that people have asked for centuries. We will address these in later chapters. For now let us ponder this truth: our sovereign God controls everything, including time and space. From the speed of the earth's orbit around the sun to the trapped fly in the spiderweb in a backyard, a wondrous God maintains ownership, interest and care in every aspect of His creation.

A shot in the dark?

God's providence is perfectly illustrated in the story of how wicked King Ahab of Israel was killed in warfare. 1 Kings 22:34–35 says:

> But a certain man drew his bow at random and struck the king of Israel between the scale armour and the breastplate. Therefore, he said to the driver of his chariot, "Turn around and carry me out of the battle, for I am wounded." And the battle continued that day, and the king was propped up in his chariot facing the Syrians, until at evening he died.

At first glance it seems the king's injury and subsequent death were random—indeed, the word "random" is used to describe the act of drawing the bow that felled Ahab. But was it? Consider these points:

- Before the battle, a prophet named of Micaiah (son of Imlah) said God had determined King Ahab would die on the battlefield.
- Because of this, King Ahab disguised himself so he would not be a target, and so, from the perspective of the Syrian enemy, he was not there, and no one was aiming an arrow in his direction.
- King Ahab had already withdrawn from the battlefield when he was shot, and was out of the fire of almost all of the arrows.
- The random arrow not only found the disguised king but hit him in the only vulnerable spot in his armour. That shot was highly unlikely.

So, was it just an arrow that went off course? Was it good luck for that nameless Syrian soldier and bad luck for King Ahab? Perhaps things were not as they seemed.

King Ahab of Israel was a wicked and unjust man. Before he entered the battle on that fateful day, the prophet named Micaiah denounced him, declaring that he would die in the upcoming battle. Upon hearing Micaiah's prophecy, Ahab threw the negative prophet into prison, to be held there until he returned safely from the battle. When he got back he planned to punish Micaiah. After all, Micaiah had said, "If you return in peace, the LORD has not spoken by me" (1 Kings 22:28).

Ahab had every expectation of escaping from this ominous prophecy. And so, instead of entering the fray, he disguised and positioned himself outside of the range of fire on the battlefield. In his mind he was perfectly safe.

But God has his own plans, always. We come back to the battle scene where the scripture says, "A certain man drew his bow at random." Perhaps the Syrian warrior was jostled by the archer shooting next to him, and it sent his arrow off course. Perhaps he misfired due to chaos and distraction around him. Perhaps he just shot arrows wherever they would go. Whatever the circumstances, this is true: God directed that arrow. He directed the way the arrow was crafted; the bow tension; the physical strength of the warrior who launched it; the velocity, arc and trajectory; the wind speed that carried it; the movement of the king at a precise moment that allowed that arrow to strike his body and hit a vital organ. God had already spoken in advance that Ahab would not survive this battle.

This random arrow took down a king. It is an incredible thought. No doubt it appeared to be a lucky arrow, a fluke shot, a one in a million chance. But we who read the biblical text have already been prepared to say that what appears random to us is not random at all. The death of King Ahab was predetermined. Let's refresh our minds as to what this means. When we speak of God's Providence, we speak of His governance of all created things.

The implications of meticulous sovereignty

Consider the implications of this: Jesus controls the atoms that make up your body, the ground under your feet, the air you breathe, the world upon which you stand and the universe in which you live. All of it is held together and directed by the Son of God. Furthermore, if Jesus were not constantly, moment by moment, sustaining all these things, the forces that hold the atoms in place would fly apart and all things would cease to be. Everything that exists—past, present and future—does so by His will and permission. Everything that goes on does so under His direction. That's what we mean when we talk about *meticulous* sovereignty.

In the story of King Ahab, the arrow that struck him down—indeed, every arrow on the battlefield—was part of his creation. The physical properties of that arrow, as well as the man who shot it, were His. The will for Ahab (who was also God's creation) to die was also the Father's will.

In Job 34:14–15 (CSB), Elihu says, "If he put his mind to it and withdrew the spirit and breath he gave, every living thing would perish together and mankind would return to the dust."

Elihu is saying that only by the permission and will of God do we live, because it is God who gives the spirit of breath and actively sustains life. The prayer of Ezra in Nehemiah 9:6 says the same:

> You are the LORD, you alone. You have made Heaven, the Heaven of Heavens, with all their host, the earth and all that is on it, the seas and all that is in them; and you preserve all of them.

Ezra uses the phrase "you preserve all of them." To preserve something is to carefully maintain it. According to Ezra, God is maintaining the sun, moon, stars and planets, the earth and all that is on it. God is the reason everything exists and inhabits space. God is the reason things continue in their present form. Were he to wish otherwise, all things would *be* otherwise.

Consider Psalm 104:29: "When you hide your face, they are dismayed; when you take away their breath, they die and return to their dust."

According to Psalm 104, our lives are dependent upon God's kind disposition towards us. Whenever God hides His face—that is, whenever God no longer wills that our lives continue—we die. Hence, we must conclude that at each moment, in each microsecond, we exist because He actively and purposely wills that we should do so.

Similarly, in 2 Peter 3:7, it says, "But by the same word the Heavens and earth that now exist are stored up for fire, being kept until the day of judgment."

"Being kept" means God has willed them to continue to exist until the judgment. Above all, this tells us that God keeps things going for a purpose. We are assured that God is not toying with His universe to keep Himself amused; God has both immediate and long-term goals for all things. In such a world there is no luck, nor are there occurrences that frustrate the Creator's purpose in creating. Hence, no matter how random an event looks to us, it does not appear that way to the Creator. To put it another way, things don't exist only by His will, but also for His purpose.

Some feel that life is a gamble, and that every time they throw the dice or make a major decision about which direction their lives will go, it is up to chance. This is a precarious way to perceive the world, especially since Proverbs 16:33 says, "The lot is cast into the lap, but its every decision is from the Lord."

Nothing in God's creation is left to chance—*nothing*.

God's direct involvement in all things

The difference between direct and indirect involvement is important. Direct involvement means that at each moment, God *directly* causes all physical actions to occur. Indirect involvement means that He created physical laws to govern all things and that He governs *indirectly* through natural phenomena, though He knows how things will turn out.

Psalm 135:7 says, "He it is who makes the clouds rise at the end of the earth, who makes lightnings for the rain and brings forth the wind from his storehouses."

Psalm 29:9 says, "The voice of the Lord makes the deer give birth and strips the forests bare, and in His temple all cry, 'Glory!'"

But what about . . . ?

Most people, even many Christians, have never given Providence much thought. They simply assume that things happen as they do, without considering the involvement of God. Others look for the hand of God only in major decisions, crisis events or natural disasters. Only when they see an extraordinary event do they consider God's involvement. But once we grasp the hand of God in *all* things, our awareness of God is stronger. But this is when questions arise, some of them extremely complex. Then, newly awakened to the true power of God, people ask such things as:

- What bearing does God's meticulous Providence have on science?
- Is God directly involved in every aspect of our solar system?
- What about free will—are our choices free? Does God really direct my choices, or do I?
- What's the difference between Providence and fatalism?
- How do I live a life filled with options when God is in control of everything?

I intend to address these questions and more in the coming chapters.

Providence means God is near

If you come, as I have done, to the conclusion that God directs all things in a meticulous hands-on way, I suspect you will never use the words "coincidence" or "luck" again. Instead, you will see the direct hand of God in all things. God is nearer than we ever believed!

CHAPTER 2

Science Under God's Hand

God acts in all ways, on all days, in the minutiae of our lives. He controls it all right down to the protons, neutrons and electrons in the atoms that make up every bit of matter. However, what is remarkable is that He is predictable in how He does this. God most often functions in the same fashion. He always causes rocks to fall towards the earth. He always causes the earth to spin on its axis. The Bible calls this "the faithfulness of God." And this is why we can study the repeated predictable patterns in nature. Because God is faithful, the scientific enterprise is possible.

However, now that the scientific enterprise is well underway, some scientists and philosophers argue that miracles, as they are described in the Bible, are not possible. The famous philosopher David Hume argued that because a miracle violated the laws of nature, they ought to be dismissed.[3] Part of his reasoning lay in the presumption that one could not substantiate a miracle through scientific investigation.

The Bible makes many claims to miracles. We have already said that when a miracle occurs, God acts outside of His predictable norms or patterns. It is not that a miracle is the intervention of God while the daily repeatable patterns of nature are not. God is always intervening. But sometimes, for his wise and eternal purposes, God chooses to act in ways that are unusual. So when a miracle occurs, nothing has changed. God is always active. The universe doesn't run itself.

---

[3] Hume, David. *An Enquiry Concerning Human Understanding.* 1748.

God moves our solar system and manages our weather

I've had many conversations with people who somehow cannot reconcile the idea of an omnipresent God with natural science. One friend said to me, "The reason I can't be a Christian is that I believe in science."

I asked him, "What do you mean?"

He said, "I believe the reason for natural phenomena can only be understood through science. We no longer need to resort to miracles to explain everything from why it rains to why the earth suddenly begins to shake violently during an earthquake. We know there are natural causes for all things. The gods are not angry. Those who believe in a sovereign God have an ever-shrinking defense for their belief, for the number of unexplained phenomena is ever shrinking."

We were then seated on an outdoor patio overlooking a wide open space with a stream in the foreground and majestic mountains in the background. I wondered whether he meant that the formations of the geography we were both admiring came as a result of the motions of tectonic plates, and not because of the command of God. He nodded.

As fascinating as that conversation might have been, I was interested in taking it in a different direction. I said, "Have a look around you. How is it that there is a landscape at all? The scientific consensus is that matter is not eternal. So there really was a time when there was no physical matter at all. It is easy to speak of the laws of nature, but these very laws once did not exist. What scientific principle explains something emerging from nothing? What scientific principle are you leaning on as you daily witness the miracle of the world around you? Is not the existence of matter itself a violation of the laws of nature?"

I am happy to report that our conversation continued through many weeks until my friend bowed the knee to Christ and surrendered his life to the one who created and sustained him. But that brings us back to our initial conversation. Scientists acknowledge that matter is not eternal, therefore the existence of something rather than nothing is the very definition of a miracle. It defies all scientific principles. "You have become fixated on miracles rather than on Providence," I tell my non-believing friends. "Furthermore, creation *itself* is a miracle."

I have said that a miracle is God acting in a way which is unusual. Imagine the experiment of dropping a rock off a tower and it falls to the earth. What if, after repeating this experiment thousands of times, on one occasion the rock lifts into space? We would call this a miracle, because the normal pattern of God's governance of nature was altered. Hence, a miracle is not God's intervention into a creation that normally functions on its own. Rather, it is an unusual and unexpected altering of the consistent and predictable patterns of the past.

Scientists notice *consistency* in nature and seek to explain it, such as a rock falling downward in the direction of the planet, rather than upward. Scientists know that, in nature, any body with sufficient mass draws objects toward its centre, and so are not surprised at the rock's behaviour. Consistent and predictable patterns occur in nature.

Providence teaches us that whether nature behaves according to its normal patterns or is unexpectedly altered, the constancy of God's hand has not changed. And so, whether we witness the unexpected in a form of a miracle or we do not, all things continue to be held together by the Sustainer.

Providence makes science possible

Science is not a threat to Christianity. Historically, Christians have embraced scientific discoveries with great interest. Science and faith are not mutually exclusive. It is not an either/or situation. The truth of the matter is that a robust doctrine of Providence has made the scientific enterprise possible. We might say that scientific observation of nature is observation of how God consistently directs it. The modern scientific enterprise initially arose out of a Christian worldview.

The history of science is rich with practicing Christians. People such as Johannes Kepler (laws of planetary motion), Galileo (earth's rotation), Sir Francis Bacon (scientific method), and Isaac Newton (gravity) were devout Christians. Christianity presented these men with a world view that made the scientific enterprise a possibility. Had they held belief in the fickle gods and goddesses of pagan religions, they would have had no groundwork to look for consistent and observable laws of nature.

We have talked about Christ holding all things together. Critics of the Christian faith argue that if it is Christ who holds all things together, that it is a supernatural, not natural, explanation of things. Unfortunately, this critique is accurate for *some* Christians. Those who have no doctrine of Providence only see the hand of God in the miraculous. They think God is there when they attend a supernatural healing service but fail to see Him as medical technology makes advancements by studying the nature of things. Although they acknowledge that God intervenes in creation, from their perspective one can only resolve the clash between science and faith by appealing to special miraculous moments—to miracles. For the one who holds to Providence, the discoveries of the natural world are also a discovery of how the faithful Creator oversees his creation. There is no conflict.

For this reason, divine Providence does not exclude scientific explanation. A Christian can believe that Christ holds all things together but still understand that there is a natural explanation for thunder, and rather than witnessing God's anger, they are witnessing what happens when a sudden increase of air pressure and temperature comes from lightning. Where Christians differ from non-believers, however, is that Christians start every exploration from the premise that *God created what they are studying*, and that they are simply revealing the patterns in His mysteries.

God is not fickle

God's patterns give us comfort, intrigue us and arouse our curiosity. God is not fickle; he does not do things on a whim. He is constant, steady and faithful. He always works for our good.

In contrast, think of a merciless dictator, one who demonstrates no reason in whether he will favour or kill you. Such a person is highly unpredictable. If he had a bad night's sleep, he might have you killed because he is feeling out of sorts; if he had a fight with a wife or mistress, he might have you flogged. Anything might set him off, and when it does all rules fly out the window.

Ancient Greek and Roman gods were like that. They were capricious and fickle. They might elevate or condemn any person they chose, for reasons unknown to human beings. In this ancient belief system, keeping up with what the gods were doing was practically impossible. It was also a convenient way to explain all manner of things. When you got sick and when you recovered, the gods had acted. If you became rich or lost your money, the gods had acted. Everything was due to the gods. You could try to appease them through offerings and sacrifice, but even if you did your best you had no assurance whether they would favour or condemn you. Those gods were simply unpredictable!

If this belief system had endured, despot gods running the affairs of the world, the scientific approach would never have evolved, because under this system nature was not predictable. There were no discernable patterns. She was fickle. Fortunately, the worldview of the Greco-Roman gods gave way to the Gospel of Jesus, and out of that a new worldview took root, which held that all those gods were merely idols —"scarecrows in a cucumber field" (Jeremiah 10:5)—and that the one true God was creator of heaven and earth.

Psalm 96:5 says: "For all the gods of the peoples are worthless idols, but the Lord made the Heavens." Deuteronomy 7:9 says: "Know therefore that the Lord your God is God, the faithful God who keeps covenant and steadfast love with those who love Him and keep His commandments, to a thousand generations."

What this means is that the one true Creator God is faithful. He commits Himself to keeping every promise He has made. He is also predictable, and His attributes remain constant. He is not righteous one day and unrighteous the next, depending on his feelings; instead, God is constantly righteous. He never acts with injustice. Indeed, Hebrews 6:18 says: "It is impossible for God to lie."

God never denies His character. He never makes a promise today and breaks it tomorrow. Consider James 1:17: "Every good gift and every perfect gift is from above, coming down from the Father of lights, with whom there is no variation or shadow due to change."

Or consider Malachi 3:6: "For I the Lord do not change." God is consistent. He is the same yesterday, today and tomorrow, and so, if this consistent, unchangeable God governs the universe, then He functions in consistent patterns and it is possible to study His Word, His character and His creation. Creation was not only made by God, but by a *consistent* God, and it follows that He governs His creation in a consistent way.

For scientific inquiry, this means that if a well-constructed experiment gives us a certain result today, it will give the same result tomorrow when repeated by someone else. This is why I argue that the modern scientific era came *out of*, and not *despite*, the Christian worldview. A consistent, reliable God not only created all things but preserves them, allowing humans—who are also part of his creation—to study His observable and repeatable patterns in the natural world. Of course, we are not required to believe in God to observe His patterns; nevertheless, God's Providence gave rise to modern science.

Psalm 19:1 says, "The Heavens declare the glory of God, and the sky above proclaims His handiwork."

Psalm 50:6 says, "The Heavens declare His righteousness, for God Himself is judge!"

What these psalms are saying is that the created universe behaves consistently because God, the altogether consistent one, sustains it. This provides a great deal of comfort for the believer, because Christians know that His Providence is kind, loving and benevolent. 1 Timothy 6:17 says that we must put our hope in God, "who richly provides us with everything to enjoy."

In Acts 17:24–25, when the apostle Paul addressed the philosophers in Athens, he said:

> The God who made the world and everything in it, being Lord of Heaven and earth, does not live in temples made by man, nor is He served by human hands, as though He needed anything, since He Himself gives to all mankind life and breath and everything.

And that's it. God not only directs arrows on the battlefield, but He also directs air to enter my lungs so that I can live, and He does so in a way that can be studied. He does these things to accomplish His mysterious and eternal purposes, and the fact that He holds all things together should be of great comfort to everyone.

CHAPTER 3

Providence Is the Purpose of His Will

Years ago, Mick Jagger of the Rolling Stones warned us in song that we can't always get what we want; but with enough effort, we can sometimes get what we need. That sounds hopeful. I may not get what I want, but I might get what I need.

Two things strike me in this song:

1) It does not promise that we will get what we need. "Sometimes" we will. At other times, we will get neither what we want nor what we need. This is the tragedy of human existence.
2) Many people do not know what they truly need. Hence, when they get it they fail to appreciate what it is they have received. Because of their lack of wisdom, the thing they need may not seem to be a blessing at all and they discard it. Further adding to the misery is the possibility that they may later realize the treasure it was. Such is the heartbreak of many lives.

At its basic level, this song is a statement on faith. We *try* in our endeavours because we believe we might achieve success. We *believe* on some level that we will. However, if our endeavours fail, a common tendency is to despair due to what we see as a lack. And yet, if we have wisdom enough, we may understand the lesson, because the lesson is what we need. The lesson is God's gift to us.

For example, perhaps during a first attempt to build a bookshelf you press the drill too hard and crack the wood. In despair, you say, "I am a terrible carpenter." Frustrated, you quit and just buy a bookshelf, thinking, *This is a waste of time.* You did not get what you wanted—a good-looking, sturdy bookshelf.

But maybe what you needed wasn't the bookshelf. Maybe you needed to learn not to press the drill too hard. Perhaps you are about to find out your wife is pregnant, and maybe in the future you will need good drill technique so you can build a playhouse for your daughter or fix a piece of siding on the house you will buy. So, what you *wanted* is short-sighted; what you *need* is God's gift to you.

It's been said that many live their lives in quiet desperation, longing for things that never arrive. To spend one's life longing for something that never arrives is a tragedy. Then, following a life lacking in both meaning and satisfaction, one dies with a sigh. Ah, the wretchedness of the human condition! Solomon seems to stray into this discussion when he said, in Proverbs 13:12, "Hope deferred makes the heart sick, but a desire fulfilled is a tree of life."

It seems the Rolling Stones had it right. The reality of life is that we may desire a great many things that don't come to pass. We don't always get what we want! Yes, on the odd occasion, if we try very hard, we may get what we need. But as Thoreau reminded us, we might not.

God always gets what He wants

While we do not always get what we want, God *always* does! Psalm 115:3 says, "Our God is in the Heavens; He does all that He pleases."

It is not that God does some of the things that he pleases. Rather, *all* that pleases God is done by God. None of God's actions end in disappointment. God is never frustrated. He is never preoccupied with unfulfilled longing. Psalm 115 compares God to idols. Idols are lifeless and powerless. They have mouths that can't speak, eyes that can't see, hands that can't feel, and feet that can't walk. In contrast, God is all powerful. What He desires always comes to pass. Always. That is the premise upon which all life rests, and upon which the message of this book rests as well.

Paul states something very similar in Ephesians 1:11. He says that God "works all things according to the counsel of His will."

This means God "works" or "causes things to happen" in the way that *He* desires. This is as it should be. God is not short-sighted. He has no shortage of power or wisdom. He does not need great effort to accomplish anything as humans do; he merely speaks, and whatever he calls into being, no matter how big or small, stands fast. God fashions and shapes everything according to his divine will and pleasure. God is always successful. God never fails. God never makes plans he is unable to bring about. God always gets what he wants. He is God.

Providence points to purpose

Part one of divine Providence presupposes meticulous sovereignty, meaning God controls both the grand events that capture our attention, as well as the minutiae. God is a micromanager who rules over all things, at each moment in time, to ensure consistency in how all things exist—and all things exist because God constantly wishes them to. He causes them to exist. Were He to turn His face away, they, and we, would immediately be no more.

Not only do all things exist at each moment in time because of God, but He also causes all things to exist *to fulfill the purpose of His will.* This is part two.

This should not be a new thought for Christians. According to Isaiah 43:7, God created human beings for his glory. Hence, human beings exist to showcase the greatness of the God who made them. We are made for God. His purpose in creating us was to externalize His perfections in the crown of His creation—men and women. We humans were created and are sustained with great and specific purpose. Of all the natural world, which is also a marvelous expression of God's creation, we are his crowning masterpiece, made in his image, created and sustained for God's purposes.

Unfortunately, a great many of us do not follow this line of reasoning to its inevitable conclusion. If we are truly created for his purpose, then God's purpose and greatness, rather than our own, is the theme of the story. Rather than finding out what we are about, our goal is to find what God is about.

Where do we start? Let's start in the Psalms (emphasis mine).

Psalm 23:2 says, "He leads me in paths of righteousness for *His name's sake.*"

Psalm 25:11 says, "*For your name's sake*, O LORD, pardon my guilt, for it is great."

Psalm 31:3 says, "For you are my rock and my fortress; and *for your name's sake* you lead me and guide me."

Psalm 79:9 says, "Help us, O God of our salvation . . . deliver us, and atone for our sins, *for your name's sake!*"

It is important to pay attention. Apart from Psalm 23, the other three examples in the Psalms come to us in the form of a prayer. We are listening as the psalmist makes his plea that God would act on his behalf. He wants forgiveness of sins. Who wouldn't? He wants directions and guidance. He also wants deliverance from trouble. In response to these requests, the psalmist learns that God is motivated not by our needs, but for the sake of His great name.

How then is this Good News? If God only acts for the sake of His great name and not ours, how can the psalmist find any comfort at all? God seems absorbed with Himself, and not with us. But this is very Good News indeed, since what the psalmist asks for are the very things that God does for the sake of His great name! God is acting, as always, for His glory. He does all things for His name's sake. And so, if the one praying aligns his requests with the purposes of God, they will be assured that they will get all they ask for. Not only will God always get what He wants, but when the one praying wants the same things as God, they also always get what they want.

This is the key to all praying. God is working out His purposes in all things. All prayer is heard when it is premised on a desire for God's glory. That's the repeated line in the Psalms: "For your name's sake." It is never "for my name's sake." No prayer is heard unless God glorifies Himself. That is why we can confidently say we are made for God. The reverse is not true. God was not made for us.

But are there no exceptions to this? At first glance, we might think there are some exceptions. For example, Isaiah 37:35 says, "For I defend this city to save it, for my own sake and for the sake of my servant David."

Here the sake of God, or the purpose of God's glorification, is paired with the words "for the sake of David." Are we to understand that God, on occasion, breaks His own rule? If the conditions are just right, will He give the same glory to David as he does to himself? And if He does that for David, might He not do certain things for the sake of the greatness of other human beings? Does God ever act for the glory of any of us?

A careful examination of Isaiah 37:35 will reveal that God *never* acts for the glory of any of us. We can say this with confidence because of the unique historical circumstances that gave rise to the kingship of David. David, Israel's great king, was explicitly told that his throne would give rise to the coming of the Messiah. After David's death, one of his ancestors would inherit his throne and rule the earth forever. Hence David stands in for the greater one to come. When Isaiah says that God does all things for His own sake and for the sake of David, he is saying that God does all things for His own sake and for the sake of His Messiah who is coming into the world. In short, Isaiah 37:35 does not promise that God adds our glory or purposes to His motivation in acting. Rather, the passage reaffirms that the glory of Jesus, the eternal Son, has equal glory to that of the eternal Father. God then acts for His glory, and His glory alone.

Furthermore, Isaiah 48:11 says, "For my sake, for my own sake, I do it, for how should my name be profaned? My glory I will not give to another."

Providence reveals the glory of God

God does all things so that his name might be highly esteemed, and, unlike us, God always gets what He wants. So what does this tell us about God's Providence? We have already made the point that God rules over all things. We also know that God continuously causes all things to exist. But now we add that when God acts, his purposes remain fixed. He is interested in proclaiming His greatness. This is His only motivation.

Some of us are offended by this thought. We protest. How can God act in such a manner? If any human being acted in this fashion, they would be rightly condemned. It is egotistical to act in this manner. But what is egotistical for humans is not egotistical for God. For in truth we are not utterly glorious. Our glory does not fill heaven and earth. When we are egotistical, we are liars. But when God acts only for the sake of His glory, He is acting on the basis of truth. For His glory fills heaven and earth. Furthermore, when in arrogance we might say to God, "Who do you think you are," God has already responded. "I think I am God. I am the Lord your God, the maker and sustainer of heaven and earth!"

Therefore, we must abandon any thought of God's motivation that is not premised on this fundamental reality: whatever God does, He acts to display the splendour of His being.

God's providential care for the earth

We can break God's governance of all things into two categories: the worlds of living and non-living things. Let's begin with non-living things. God places the mountains precisely where they are because that arrangement most highlights His glory. The existence and placement of fertile valleys—or rivers, trees, rocks, deserts—best serve His purpose. That the earth is an orb in which some parts of it experience different climactic conditions from others is a decision made by God. I live in a part of the world where winter is rainy, dark and gloomy because God decided it should be so. In ways known only to Him, He is glorified by this.

Psalm 135:6–7 says, "Whatever the LORD pleases, he does, in heaven and on earth, in the seas and all deeps. He it is who makes the clouds rise at the end of the earth, who makes lightnings for the rain, and brings forth the wind from His storehouses."

Translation: you don't like the weather? It didn't happen that way by accident. God designs each day down to the details. Every day He does the things he most desires.

Allow me to illustrate. One wintery Sunday morning years ago I was on my way to church, where I served as senior pastor. As was my custom, I awoke early, got dressed and prepared to leave for the church so I could arrive early to study, pray and commit the Sunday morning worship to the grace of God. Included in my prayers was a request that my sermon accurately reflect the scripture and speak truth and consolation to those who needed it.

Winters in my city are relatively mild. I live just outside Vancouver, and the proximity of the Pacific Ocean allows for a warmer air than is felt in the rest of Canada. While it snows freely in the interior provinces each winter, it mostly rains on the Pacific Coast. *Mostly* rains. On this winter's day, I awakened to a thick coat of snow on the ground.

I knew what that meant: church attendance was going to be down. The wet snow we experience in Greater Vancouver is often quite slippery and prone to freezing, making driving a test of nerves. Furthermore, Vancouver's many hills add another element of danger, so unless it is absolutely necessary, Vancouverites stay home in such conditions.

As I drove, I prayed. It was not a prayer of faith, or for God's glory. It was a prayer of complaint before God. I prayed, "I know why it snowed last night. It snowed because you made it snow. And you know that when you make it snow on Saturday night in Vancouver, very few people show up in church on Sunday morning. Why would you do that? Why can't you make it snow on Sunday night, or Wednesday night, or any other night? There are six other nights you could have chosen, but you frequently bring snow on Saturday nights. Saturday night! Don't you *want* people to show up for church?"

Basically, I was annoyed. I wanted God to know that, while I understood His providential care over the earth, I didn't like spending a week getting ready for a great company of people, only to find the room empty after all that preparation. I was bitter. And then, as I drove the snowy freeway with great care, something happened that I have only experienced a few times in my life: I heard God's voice. I heard Him say, "Would you question my governance, as well as my ordering of the world I have created for *myself*? I sent this snow on Saturday night for *my own* sake and not for yours. Would you question me?"

I became quiet. My praying ceased. I realized I needed to do two things: repent and commit to *praising* rather than *complaining*.

Carefully read the words of Psalm 104:10-15:

> You make springs gush forth in the valleys; they flow
> between the hills; they give drink to every beast of

the field; the wild donkeys quench their thirst. Beside them the birds of the Heavens dwell; they sing among the branches. From your lofty abode you water the mountains; the earth is satisfied with the fruit of your work. You cause the grass to grow for the livestock and plants for man to cultivate, that he may bring forth food from the earth and wine to gladden the heart of man, oil to make his face shine and bread to strengthen man's heart.

When God orders His creation for His own good purposes, we are the beneficiaries of His blessing. The snow that fell that Saturday night was a part of God's ordering of the seasons. The regular order of the seasons bolsters the fertile farmland near where I live. Winter hydrates the land and lets it rest. When spring comes, the land is moist, fertile and ready for planting, so that after a warm summer growing season, there is bountiful harvest in the fall. In this way God is glorified and we are blessed. God's glory and our good are of one piece.

Consider the words of Thomas Chisholm's "Great Is Thy Faithfulness," Verse 2: "Summer and winter, and springtime and harvest, sun, moon, and stars in their courses above join with all nature in manifold witness to Thy great faithfulness, mercy and love."[4]

Mature Christians worship and rejoice in God's wisdom, compelled by the providential care inherent in the world around them. Rather than complaining about too much rain, snow or sunshine, we need to see that each day presents an opportunity to view the hand of God, who is actively arranging this day for His glory. Whenever we complain, it is a complaint against God, who specifically created that day. The weather is not an accident, it is a part of God's providential design. Why not admire how we are sustained by the seasons and the weather?

Job 37:6 records Elihu saying, "For to the snow he says, 'fall on the earth,' likewise to the downpour, his mighty downpour."

Yes, it is God's snow. Yes, it is God's rain. Do you view the weather as a daily illustration of God's Providence? Are you amazed at His rulership of the earth? If not, perhaps it's time to consider this. Stop and

---

[4] Chisholm, Thomas. "Great Is Thy Faithfulness." 1923.

notice His hand at work, and then give God glory and praise for His Providence in the natural world. Marvel at the work of His hands and notice that He orders His world according to the purpose of His will.

God's Providence over living things

Let's move from the inanimate world to the world of living things. Jesus spoke directly to how the ability of birds to find food, and the abundance of it, is directed by God. In Matthew 6:26 he says, "Look at the birds of the air: they neither sow nor reap nor gather into barns, and yet your Heavenly Father feeds them."

In Matthew 10:29, Jesus comments on the faithfulness of God's care, as he points out that the lifespan of even the smallest creatures are subject to God's eternal plan: "Are not two sparrows sold for a penny? And not one of them will fall to the ground apart from your Father."

Isn't that fascinating? A mayfly lives just one day. The average housefly lives for three days. A giant tortoise can live over 170 years. By the way, that's one of the reasons I won't get one as a pet. It would outlive my great-grandchildren! What a thing to pass down in your will!

God not only arranges the lifespan of each of His creatures, but He also arranges for their food, designs their physical and mental capabilities and oversees the unique circumstances that govern their lives. He does the same with us, the crown of his creation.

Immediate and ultimate causes

The idea of things in nature occurring randomly is popular in the secular community, but Christians who do not accept the idea of divine providence can sometimes feel this way as well. To such people, I would like to point out that it is wise to distinguish between "immediate cause" and "ultimate cause." An immediate cause is the direct, obvious cause of an incident or event. The ultimate cause is events or conditions that made the immediate cause possible.

Here is a great example. Let's say your young son hits his classmate. You are understandably upset and determine that it's time to give him a well-deserved lecture. You begin your inquisition with a question: "Why did you do that?" You expect him to say, "He was bugging me and has been making me angry all week long! He teased me, called me names, stole my lunch and I finally had enough."

Probably you were expecting an answer like that, and you were prepared to give him options on handling anger and injustice in a non-violent way. As a good Christian parent, you were aware that these are valuable life lessons your son needs to learn.

But what if he says, "I hit him because my Creator fashioned me to experience emotions. Had I no capacity to experience emotions this would never have occurred. Also, you taught me to believe all things are sustained by God, so how can you ask me why I hit Billy when Billy not only had it coming, but it was God's design that his reckoning would come at the end of my fist?"

What would you say to your son if he said *that*?

Even while you might agree that the human capacity to experience emotion is a wonderful gift of God, you would likely find yourself taking on the parenting tone and saying, "Don't change the subject! You know *exactly* what I was asking you! And it was *not* for you to engage me in a theological discussion!"

And surely your son *did* know what you were asking—you were asking him the immediate cause for his actions, and he responded with the ultimate cause.

There is a lot to think about in this example. It is true your son was made to experience emotion. It is also true that your son is subject to Adam's sin. However, the same can be said of his classmates, and every human on this planet. All of us are under the sovereign control of God. This is a great discussion to have with him, and you should congratulate him on his clever theological discourse—but perhaps you should discipline him first!

Ultimately, all things are caused by God, and God oversees all things. He has purpose and dominion, even if some of what occurs on this earth—injustice, heartbreak, injury, untimely death, crime and even punishment—are uncomfortable, trying and sometimes even soul-crushing. To God, pressure upon us turns us from coal to diamonds and brings us closer to the perfection that He is. In this way we are tested; however, God is not the author of evil. That proposition will be discussed later.

For now, let's limit our study to the immediate, physical cause of falling snow on the Saturday before Sunday worship. The immediate cause was because a frigid Arctic outflow pushed down from the north. The ultimate cause was because God wanted it to snow that night for reasons of His own.

Providence harmonizes the big and small

Some Bible teachers talk about the "doctrine of concurrence," which holds that God directs and does His work through the distinctive properties of each created thing so that these things themselves bring about the results that we see. In this way it is possible to affirm that all events are caused by both God *and* nature, with nature as the immediate cause and God as the ultimate cause.

How does this compare to divine Providence in scripture? In Job 38, as part of a wider passage in which God is questioning Job, God tries to help Job recognize the limits of his wisdom and consider the vast sum of God's wisdom as ruler of creation. Job 38:39–41 says:

> Can you hunt the prey for the lion, or satisfy the appetite of the young lions, when they crouch in their dens or lie in wait in their thicket? Who provides for the ravens its prey, when its young ones cry to God for help, and wander about for lack of food?

Are you surprised at that language? Have you ever seen documentary footage that shows a lion hunting down prey and killing it? God says the appetite of the lion and the successful hunt that satisfies it are both his creations. And the ravens? They cry out to him for food. God says their only hope for being fed comes from him, even though ravens are not created in the image of God and thus don't know him.

Let's go forward to Job 39:13–17:

> The wings of the ostrich wave proudly, but are they the pinions and plumage of love? For she leaves her eggs to the earth and lets them be warmed on the ground, forgetting that a foot may crush them and that the wild

beast may trample them. She deals cruelly with her young, as if they were not hers; though her labour be in vain, yet she has no fear, because God has made her forget wisdom and given her no share in understanding.

God designed this animal. God is the cause of the ostrich's lack of sense. "Listen," says God, "the reason ostriches are as dumb as they are is because it pleased me to make them exactly that way." At least the ostrich puts his or her head in the sand when in danger—sheep have no self-defence mechanisms at all! They are picked off by predators without even putting up a fight.

God's creatures are myriad and mysterious. God designed leopards to hunt and wildebeests to be hunted. He designed vultures to clean up carcasses that lie on the earth. All these things are His ideas, and all these creatures are, in some way, serving His eternal purpose. The earth is not the product of accident, but of wisdom of the one who made all things for His glory.

Carefully read Proverbs 6:6–9:

> Go to the ant, O sluggard; consider her ways, and be wise. Without having any chief, officer, or ruler, she prepares her bread in summer and gathers her food in harvest. How long will you lie there, O sluggard? When will you arise from your sleep?

In the natural world God has given us numerous illustrations of His grace and provided us with His warnings. He uses natural order to teach us of Himself and to declare His splendour. From ants we learn the importance of industry. From ostriches we learn how foolish it is to hide from our problems. From sheep we learn the importance of following our shepherd. From snakes we are warned of deceit and death.

The scriptures, which are God's final word to us, do not come in a vacuum. They come to us in the context of the world God has made. That context is almost always within the natural world, which was created by God in such a way that we can understand His truth. The natural world and the Bible were both created exactly as they are to best communicate God's glory to us. God meticulously designed it that way.

The Creator is involved both in the world and in our lives, every moment of every day. How foolish when we only see His hand in miracles, for His hand is all around us all the time. God speaks in creation and directs the properties of every created thing, both living and non-living. He not only causes them to exist and is responsible for their existence, but He also gives purpose to all that is. Yes, it really *is* true that all things are caused by God, for the purpose of His glory!

CHAPTER 4

God Rules the Nations

My parents grew up in small German-speaking villages in what was then part of the Union of Soviet Socialist Republics (USSR). Both their villages were in what is now within the nation of Ukraine.

Their growing-up years were ones of terror. Joseph Stalin ruled the Soviet Union with an iron fist and, under Soviet Marxism, divided the people into two classes. Landowning capitalists who owned the means of production were called "bourgeoisies." These were the enemies of the state. The second, larger group, the workers, were called the "proletariat." These were the industrial workers, who sold their labour to the bourgeoisies. It was the proletariat that were called upon to rise up and overthrow the oppression of the bourgeoisies.

But there was a group that did not easily fall into either one of these categories. These were landowning peasants, some of whom had become quite wealthy. These wealthy landowning peasants came to be known as the "kulaks." Some of the kulaks had hired labour from among the poorer of the peasants. This term was used to describe people who were also the enemies of the state. Stalin decided that the farmers in Ukraine, such as my family, were kulaks. Of course, since they owned their own farms, kulaks resisted communist collectivization.

Between the years 1928 and 1940, all peasant farms were replaced by collectivized, state-owned farms. To accomplish this many thousands of kulaks were murdered by the government. Furthermore, Stalin planned to starve out these communities, resulting in millions of deaths. In a land where topsoil was rich and food could be grown in abundance, kulaks now lived on farms that had been confiscated from them. Food was denied them. Any kulak who even stripped grain from the fields to feed his starving family was considered an enemy of the state and a counterrevolutionary. They starved to death in the midst of a land overflowing with food.

My grandfather was arrested as a counterrevolutionary. The communist police entered their home and simply took him away while my father and his siblings wept in terror. My grandmother never saw her husband again. From the best accounts our family has, he was repeatedly beaten and left outside in the bitter cold to die of the elements. But that was not the only tragedy to befall my family. One of my father's siblings, my uncle, died of malnutrition.

Eventually my parents escaped from the Soviet Union by following the retreating German army. In 1954 they arrived in Canada and settled in the Fraser Valley. I grew up as a Canadian but heard many stories from Mom and Dad about their childhoods filled with fear and terror. Whenever communist agents entered the villages, everyone was afraid. Members of the village were often recruited to betray others. Arrests often followed. No one knew whom to trust.

I relate this so that it might be apparent that I do not approach the matter of God's providential, loving, meticulous sovereignty through rose-coloured glasses; if anything, the glasses I wear are coloured by the blood of my ancestors. My grandfather was tortured to death, my father was beaten in school for refusing to say there was no God and my parents suffered all their lives from the trauma of their early years. Today we would say they suffered from PTSD.

I have often thought of my father as a little boy, refusing to renounce God even while knowing the beating it would bring. I have often thought of the praying hands of my grandmother, a widow with no means to feed eight children. When the food in the house was gone she would gather her children in a circle, and they would pray. And God was gracious to her; she testified to this until the end of her life. During those terrible years, on more than one occasion strangers left food at her door—and seven of her eight children lived into old age.

Despite what happened to her husband, to her dying day my grandmother believed in God's gracious provision. If she were beside me now as I write about God's divine Providence, I believe she would affirm every line. She experienced the goodness of the Lord. I was with her on one occasion, when in Canada she unexpectedly came upon the man who had arrested her husband. She told him she knew who he was and remembered the harm he had done. She also told him that in the name of Jesus she now forgave him and wished that he would seek God. She was a woman at peace with the hand of God in days of great suffering and profound evil.

Even evil is under God's hand

Until now we have discussed the sustaining hand of God, but human beings live in a world that is beset by great evil. If a loving Jesus sustains all things at each moment of time, why is this so?

Christians believe in the doctrine of common grace. Jesus taught that God makes His sun rise on the evil *and* the good (Matthew 5:45). He causes much-needed rain to fall on the just and unjust alike. God blesses an unworthy humanity every day with things we often take for granted—a full refrigerator, warm water, a soft bed, transportation, paved roads, including in many cases providing stable government with just laws. These are examples of what we in the Western world enjoy daily, think about very little and probably deserve even less. This is the goodness of God to people who have not responded in gratefulness. Yet God is good to all.

Yet historically there has been so much torment in the world. Here are some notable examples that come to us from the last century, which has just passed:

- In the early part of the twentieth century, some 2 million Armenian Christians died at the hands of the Ottoman Turks, a holocaust which is denied by the oppressors to this day.
- Stalin not only killed kulaks, but caused the deaths of an estimated 20 million people through Gulag camps and deportation.
- The decade-long Chinese Cultural Revolution launched by Mao Zedong in 1966 claimed the lives of more than 40 million.

- The terrors of Nazi Germany have been well documented.
- From 1975 to 1978, the Cambodian death toll of the Khmer Rouge resulted in the death of some 2 million people, roughly 25 percent of the entire population.
- The 1994 genocide in Rwanda saw 800,000 Tutsi people killed in 100 days by Hutu extremists.

Occasionally I meet people who are convinced that the world is slowly getting better; after all, there is less war on the world stage than ever before. But are the hearts of human beings really changing? It may be that, in His mercy, God permits long periods of protracted peace between separate nations. This, however, is due to His goodness and not the moral advancement of humankind. We are as deeply fallen and sinful as ever. The horrors to which the human heart is capable seems to know no bounds.

Evil remains. And this gives rise to the most basic of questions. Are we saying too much when we say that God rules the nations? And yet, Psalm 22:28 confidently asserts: "For kingship belongs to the LORD, and he rules over the nations."

Professing that Jesus is Lord is fundamental to the Christian faith. We proclaim His sovereignty and acknowledge that He rules all things. In 1 Timothy 1:17, the Christian confession that Jesus Christ is Lord asserts that he rules: "To the King of the ages, immortal, invisible, the only God, be honour and glory forever and ever. Amen."

However, there is no denying that terrible things happen in this world, and the big question is this: if God rules everything, from the atoms we are made of to the solar system and beyond, why is there such evil?

Some theologians explain evil by painting God as a being that is less than all-powerful. In the book *God at War*,[5] Jeffrey Boyd argues that the reason for suffering and evil is that God is at war with Satan. According to Boyd, God will eventually win, but he cannot win immediately. Eventually he will. But the power of Satan is great and God needs time to win the war. This is supposed to exonerate God from culpability in human suffering. But does it?

---

[5]   Boyd, Gregory. *God at War*. Intervarsity Press, 1997.

No, it does not, nor does the Bible speak this way. There is no war or government that is out of God's control. Indeed, so absolutely does the Bible depict God's unlimited power that Psalm 115 says that God does whatever He pleases. We will deal with this issue of evil later in the book.

The Apostle Paul believed in God's providence completely. He was in a prison in Rome, waiting to be tried before Caesar's tribunal. He was on trial to ascertain whether his Gospel incited treason against Rome and was a hindrance to the peace of the Empire. The result of his trial would bring him exoneration or execution. Yet in in his writings about this event, Paul never refers to it as "an unfortunate turn of events." Instead, he refers to himself as "Christ's prisoner" (Ephesians 3:1). He believed he was in prison because Christ had willed that he should be there.

Paul remained committed to God's purpose even while incarcerated. Chained daily to Caesar's elite guards, he used the opportunity to spread the Gospel. Soon the Good News spread through Caesar's household. In Philippians, Paul points out that had he not been imprisoned, the Roman praetorium (special forces, who were guarding him) and Caesar's household would never have heard the Gospel. To him, it was divine Providence that he should be chained to guards who would come to know the saving love of Christ. To him, Christ had arranged it precisely in that fashion and therefore his suffering was directed by Christ.

It's not just the polls, but Providence

In the wealthy democratic Western world in which I live, complaining about the government is practically a sport. I know, I have played this game myself. But in a world ruled by God, each election is won or lost at his pleasure.

Romans 13:1 says, "For there is no authority except from God, and those that exist have been instituted by God."

Those of us who live in the world's democracies often struggle with the premise that the government in power was appointed by God. Does God appoint the governments that we voted against? But minor policy differences are not what Christians struggle with. It is the great evil that is done by democratically elected leaders. I live in a nation with no prohibitions on abortions. Over 80,000 unborn children have their lives taken from them every year. This is a profound evil. And yet, it is the policy of democratically elected leaders.

Furthermore, the practice of allowing for medical professions to assist in suicides has also become legal. In a number of reported cases, Canadian forces veterans, struggling with trauma-recovery and PTSD, were offered medical assistance in suicide should they want to choose that option. Indeed, in one case a combat veteran claimed he was called by his case worker offering assistance in suicide. *The National Post*, in November of 2022, reported the case worker even told him that there were other occasions where individuals were offered suicide. And it is not just the government. The Angus Reed polling organization, in February of 2023, found that 61 percent of Canadians support the idea of offering medical suicide, under certain conditions, to those who are not facing imminent death. We have become a culture in love with death.[6]

Evil pervades all nations. And if this is so in democratic nations, what do we make of those nations that frequently arrest their own citizens for their religious beliefs or their unwillingness to follow unjust laws? There are to this day concentration camps inoffensively called "re-education camps," where totalitarian governments send citizens who will not comply with their demands.

I raise these matters so that when we proclaim Jesus as Lord of the nations, we take evil into account. It does no good to make religious statements about Christ's lordship of the nations without examining how that lordship works in the present era.

The biblical case for God's kingship

Nations make laws that may not be in keeping with God's laws. Since this is so, is it too much to say that God rules the nations? And yet, Psalm 22:27–28 insists it is so:

> All the ends of the earth shall remember and turn to the
> LORD, and all the families of the nations shall worship

---

[6]   Angus Reid Institute. "Cardus: Mental Health and Maid: Canadians Question Looming Changes to Canada's Assisted-Death Law." February 13, 2023.

before you. For kingship belongs to the LORD, and he
rules over the nations.

In the First Testament, kingship simply refers to the kind of
government of all the nations around Israel. We might properly apply
this verse by saying that government of the nations belong to the Lord.
This means the Lord controls the actions of rulers on the throne. We see
this principle worked out when God hardens Pharaoh's heart in Exodus.
We further see this worked out in Isaiah 37:29, where the prophet says
that God put a hook into the nose of the Assyrian King Sennacherib
and led him back to his own land. Indeed, Isaiah will even look into
the future and speak of a king not yet born. Isaiah 44:28 refers to the
coming King Cyrus, who will be the pagan ruler over the mighty Persian
Empire. Isaiah, speaking for God, says, "Cyrus, he is my shepherd and
he shall fulfill all my purpose."

We might then properly say that God exercises dominion over the
ones he has put in power. God does not rule *some* of the nations. He
rules all nations at all points in history. Our immediate reaction is that
we doubt that it can be so. But before we answer how it can be so, let's
firmly establish that the scripture claims that it is indeed so.

Deuteronomy 32:8 says:

> When the Most High gave to the nations their
> inheritance, when he divided mankind, he fixed the
> borders of the peoples according to the number of the
> sons of God.

To understand this passage, we have to imagine the scene when
Moses gives his farewell address to Israel. Moses is then aware he will
soon die. After his death, Joshua will lead Israel.

Imagine Moses on his deathbed giving his farewell address to Israel
and handing over leadership of the Israelite tribes to his assistant,
Joshua, who is to lead them to the Promised Land. They will conquer
their enemies. The boundaries of their land will soon be apportioned
out by God. But this is not his only thought.

To prepare them for this mission, Moses wants Israel to understand the neighbourhood into which they are moving. The neighbourhood is not a mere happenstance. Moses wants Israel to understand that groups of the earth receive the boundaries of their land because of the predetermined plan of God. When Moses says, "according to the sons of God," he means to say that God had already determined Israel's neighbours. Furthermore, those neighbours would play a vital role in fulfilling God's purpose for his people.

We need to remember the consequence of this arrangement. In time, Israel became involved in some bloody warfare with some of those nations, who also tried to subvert them, entice them into idolatry and cause Israel to incite the anger of God. In fact, it was Israel's observation of these bordering nations that led many of them to reject the idea of being the unique people of God. This is when they appealed to Samuel, the last of Israel's judges, "Give us a king so that we can be like those nations." Consider the implications! God was aware of how the nations he placed next to them would impact them.

How do we understand God's geographical positioning for Israel? We might rightly conclude that the boundaries he established would present Israel with the great choice: will they, as a people, trust in the Lord and cling to Him? Or will they abandon God and become like surrounding nations? God's providential determination put Israel to the test to determine what was truly in its heart.

The time of Joshua is followed by the time of the Judges. This is a time in Israel's history in which the Israelites were found to be particularly faithless. This happens not once, but many times. Consider Judges 2:20–23:

> So the anger of the LORD was kindled against Israel, and he said, "Because this people have transgressed my covenant that I commanded their fathers and have not obeyed my voice, I will no longer drive out before them any of the nations that Joshua left when he died, in order to test Israel by them, whether they will take care to walk in the way of the LORD as their father did or

not." So, the LORD left those nations, not driving them out quickly.

Here the wording is plain. The nations within the boundaries of Israel were to test Israel. Some of those nations were powerful and threatening. Their presence exposed the true state of their hearts by making the choice plain. Would Israel say, as in Psalm 63, that the loving kindness of the Lord is better than life, or would they capitulate to the idols of the nations? Over and over again, Israel is found to capitulate. Their neighbours exposed the inner recesses of their hearts. God had determined it would be so.

We are now ready to form some conclusions as to how God rules evil nations, as well as the impact they have. Psalm 46:8–10 says:

> Come, behold the works of the LORD, how he has brought desolations on the earth. He makes wars cease to the end of the earth; he breaks the bow and shatters the spear; he burns the chariots with fire. Be still and know that I am God. I will be exalted among the nations; I will be exalted in the earth!

The Psalm tells us that he orders nations in such a way that when his work is done, he will be exalted and glorified. Nations rise and fall at God's specific command. They win battles and rise to prominence, and they lose battles when God so commands. Wars break out. Peace rules at other times. God fulfills his purpose in this. He is glorified!

Job 12:23 says, "He makes nations great, and He destroys them; he enlarges nations, and leads them away."

Paul said something very similar when he spoke to the philosophers in Athens. It is recorded in Acts 17:26: "And he made from one man every nation of mankind to live on all the face of the earth, having determined allotted periods and the boundaries of their dwelling place."

This means that the exact borders of nations, as well as the predetermined period for their existence, are not determined by chance or by political reasons, *but by God Himself.* Paul went on to say that this ordering of things would lead many to "feel their way toward Him."

God so designs the development of nations that he will maximize the number of men and women who find God through Christ. Can there be any doubt that it is clear in Scripture that what happens within and among the nations is ruled by God?

God's goals are eternal

Our eternal God doesn't play the short game of small advantages; instead, he plays the long game. To focus only on how God can allow cruelty at a given moment is to not allow for the vision of the great, grand, eternal plans of God. In the course of this study, we will reaffirm that God is never the author of the evil. But he does allow their evil for a time. We will also make the case there is a difference between immediate and ultimate causes of all things. For the sake of eternal good, God allows evil its brief day.

This was brought home to me when I once stood in the city square of Timisoara, Romania. Nicolae Ceaușescu ruled that country from 1965 to 1989. He was cruel. During his time a great many people suffered and were put to death for offending him. The prisons were constantly full. But in 1989, courageous people gathered to protest his attempt to remove a faithful Christian pastor from his church. Ceaușescu responded in wrath, ordering his troops to shoot to kill protesters in the town square. Hundreds of innocent people died, including little children. It was a great horror. But the Christian man who took me to the city square where the horror had occurred did not question the wisdom of God. Rather, he pointed out that the demise of the dictator that followed that atrocity led to the revival of the church, and many finding their way to Christ.

The blood of these martyrs, though terrible in scope, was not the end of this story. After his reign, communism fell in Romania. I was given the opportunity to teach a class in a Christian university that was built in Oradea. Nurses and doctors were sent to villages that did not previously have access to health care. I also spent time with a group of young seminarians. On that occasion, we met in the very building that had once been used to train young communists.

Still, one might protest, why was it necessary for that nation to suffer as it did? The answer might be that there are times when God deliberately removes His restraining hand. That is to say, the world is far more wicked than we can imagine. The real question is not why there is so much evil, but why there is so much good. God is always and at each moment preventing a superabundance of evil that would destroy all life on earth. But He allows evil to be felt in greater abundance than at other times. Why?

I believe God allows foretastes of both heaven and hell to be felt in this world, and that he does this so that we might consider our ways. He wants us to know the outcome of moral evil as well as the outcome of righteousness. At times the shocking nature of the human heart, and what is possible in a society, causes people to turn to God, crying out for both His mercy as well as His presence. God's governance of the nations is for such things. God does not play the short game of small advantages, He plays the long game of eternal good.

If God rules the nations, then . . .

No government or nation can come into being if God does not will it to be so. I have acknowledged there is a certain mystery to this. For on the one hand, God has allowed the nations to rebel against Him. And yet in their rebellion He controls them, determining both their rise and fall. Some Christians in the West bitterly disagree with this and cannot acknowledge that whatever political party was put into power, or that took power by military force, was put there by God. But it is a biblical truth.

Consider the story of Daniel. In either 587 or 586 B.C., Nebuchadnezzar II, king of Babylonia, destroyed the small rebellious Kingdom of Judah, deporting its population and burning its temple to the ground. Daniel, a noble Jewish youth, was taken into captivity to serve the king. While in captivity he is called upon to interpret one of the king's dreams. The dream featured a huge statue of a man with a head of gold, chest and arms of silver, belly and thighs of bronze, legs of iron and feet partly of iron and partly of baked clay. A supernatural rock destroys it, and the rock becomes a mountain.

Daniel, who had remained true to the God of Israel during his captivity, called upon Him for interpretation. God explained that the statue represented a series of kingdoms, each less glorious than the one before. Nebuchadnezzar's was the gold head, and subsequent kingdoms would decline as depicted by the statue's composition. Ultimately, all earthly kingdoms would be replaced by God with one that could never be destroyed.

The Bible records Daniel's conclusion to this matter. Verse 21 says, "He changes times and seasons; He removes kings and sets up kings."

Daniel was certain that God's message to him was that Nebuchadnezzar, the enemy of his people, had been given that season of rulership by God Himself. The Bible is even more specific. Isaiah 37 says that God will not only determine the rise and fall of nations, but also who the human rulers will be, indicating that, in His providential design, God also determines what those individual rulers will do.

Isaiah 37 is an important chapter in the Bible. It details the Assyrian invasion of Jerusalem under cruel King Sennacherib. Sennacherib surrounded Jerusalem during the days when it was ruled by righteous King Hezekiah. At the height of the crisis, King Hezekiah pleaded with God for mercy. Isaiah the prophet is then called to bring God's words about Sennacherib to Hezekiah. Isaiah's words from God were:

> Have you not heard that I determined it long ago? I planned from days of old what now I bring to pass, that you should make fortified cities crash into heaps of ruins, while their inhabitants, shorn of strength, are dismayed and confounded, and have become like plants of the field and like tender grass, like grass on the housetops, blighted before it is grown [Isaiah 37:26–27].

Does that surprise you? Are you shocked that the expansion of the Assyrian Empire and its terrorizing of the nations around it was planned by God? Why did God arrange the rise of a cruel empire? The answer is because it was part of God's long-term designs.

God would call on King Hezekiah to lead his nation to repentance and revival. They had rejected the God who sustained them, leading to this crisis. Prophets of God had warned them of this, and yet their forefathers had refused to repent. Hezekiah, remembering the prophets and hearing God's promise for mercy, led the people to God in repentance. God sent His angel and put to death 185,000 Assyrian warriors, displaying His power to both Israel and Assyria. Assyria and its king served God's purposes.

But God didn't always will that Jerusalem would escape destruction. The next empire to attack them after Assyria was Babylon, and God did not strike down the Babylonian army as He did the Assyrian one; instead, the Babylonians utterly defeated Jerusalem and burned her temple to the ground, slaughtering and exiling many people. One might wonder what good came of that. Jeremiah the prophet, in the book of Lamentations 3:20–22, said:

> I well remember them, and my soul is downcast within
> me. Yet this I call to mind and therefore I have hope:
> Because of the Lord's great love we are not consumed,
> for his compassions never fail.

Jeremiah is saying, "If we have faith, though we are judged in our rebellion against God, God will show mercy." And God did show mercy to Jerusalem. The destruction of Jerusalem led the Jewish people to utterly reject idols and false gods and goddesses and to remember their covenant with God. Babylonian captivity killed Israel's love of idols. Ultimately, the return to the Promised Land would lead to the coming of Jesus and the message He would bring.

God does play the long game! But God's dealings with all nations— past, present and future—are always for the good of His church. All things, from geopolitical structures to local politics, are providentially arranged to maximize the harvest of those who would become followers of Jesus Christ. Carefully read Ephesians 1:22: "And [God the Father] put all things under [God the Son's] feet and gave him as head over all things to the church."

The context of that verse is this: when Christ was raised from the dead, the Father gave the Son authority, power and dominion over his church.

In Revelation 1:5, John calls Jesus "the ruler of kings on earth." Revelation 4:1–6 says:

> After this I looked, and behold, a door standing open in Heaven! And the first voice, which I had heard speaking to me like a trumpet, said, "Come up here, and I will show you what must take place after this." At once I was in the Spirit, and behold, a throne stood in Heaven, with one seated on the throne. And he who sat there had the appearance of jasper and carnelian, and around the throne was a rainbow that had the appearance of an emerald. Around the throne were twenty-four thrones, and seated on the thrones were twenty-four elders, clothed in white garments, with golden crowns on their heads. From the throne came flashes of lightning, and rumblings and peals of thunder, and before the throne were burning seven torches of fire, which are the seven spirits of God, and before the throne there was as it were a sea of glass, like crystal.

What is it that John is seeing? He is seeing the one on that Heavenly throne who rules over all other thrones.

Do you still need more proof? Hear the words of the pagan Persian King Cyrus. He allowed Israel to leave the land of exile and go back to their promised land. Ezra 1:2 records him saying, "The LORD, the God of Heaven, has given me all the kingdoms of the earth, and he has charged me to build him a house at Jerusalem."

What is our response?

We have established that God rules the nations, and that the nations often rage against God. God, in Providence, establishes and enacts all things, including how long a nation will stand, where borders lie, each successive monarch or leader and what that leader will do during his or her rule. Furthermore, God does this to advance the Gospel and to grow His church.

But does anything about this change our lives? Indeed it does! Once we believe in God as the ruler of all, *everything* changes! For example, those of us who live in democracies often speak well of prime ministers and presidents with whom we agree, but rage against those with whom we don't. When we feel that the wrong leader has come to power, some of us are launched into a crisis of faith, displaying a lack of faith as we react to the situation and then refusing to pray for those in power. But what we are not considering is that *there is no authority except that which is instituted by God*. We lack thankfulness for political leaders, resist those who have come into power and, in doing so, disrespect our God who put those leaders there.

As Christians we should know better. Instead of cursing leaders we dislike, why don't we begin praying in faith? What if we prayed, "Oh Lord, I know this is your doing, and that no purpose of yours can be thwarted. I don't know how but, dear Lord, as you providentially guide the nations—including my own—may this turn of events serve to advance the Gospel of Jesus Christ. For I have come to believe that the best thing that can happen in this world is not for my political philosophy to succeed, but for your Gospel to be proclaimed as widely as possible. Oh Lord, use this government to inadvertently enlarge your Church and cause even more to come to a saving knowledge of God through Christ. Amen."

Please remember that saying that God rules the nations does not mean we *approve* of what nations or their rulers do; instead, it means we acknowledge that God does all things for His purposes, always. When wicked King Sennacherib of Assyria turned the cities of the ancient world into piles of rubble, this was an evil deed. When I point out that God rules all the actions of world rulers, that does not give tacit approval to their evil deeds; it means that even evil rulers serve God.

Luther once said that even the devil himself is nothing more than the unwilling servant of God. God is not the author of evil, but God will use evil for his purposes.

CHAPTER 5

God Rules Every Human Life

Maltbie Babcock (1858–1901) was a pastor. He served first in a church in Lockport, New York, and then at Brown Memorial Presbyterian Church in Baltimore, Maryland. After his death his wife published several of his poems. The one we know best today was made into a hymn. It is called *This Is My Father's World.*[7]

By all accounts, Pastor Babcock was an outdoorsman. The first verse of *This is My Father's World* goes as so:

> *This is my Father's world, and to my listening ears, all nature sings, and round me rings the music of the spheres. This is my Father's world: I rest me in the thought of rocks and trees, of skies and seas, His hand the wonders wrought.*[8]

In the second verse, Babcock moves from the inanimate world to the world of creatures:

> *This is my Father's world: the birds their carols raise, the morning light, the lily white declare their Maker's praise.*

---

[7] Babcock, Maltbie. "This Is My Father's World." 1901.
[8] Ibid

*This is my Father's world: He shines in all that's fair;
in the rustling grass I hear Him pass; He speaks to me
everywhere.[9]*

He tackles more difficult issues in the third verse:

*This is my Father's world: Oh, let me ne'er forget that
though the wrong seems oft so strong, God is the ruler
yet.[10]*

What makes these words interesting is that Babcock seems to have
had difficulty integrating these words into what was for him a difficult
life. Early in his life he struggled with mental illness, then, while in his
early forties, he became ill with a bacterial infection while on a trip to
the Holy Land and experienced intense muscle pain, confusion and
a high fever. His mental illness returned, and in May of 1901 Maltbie
Babcock committed suicide. He slit his wrists and ingested poison. The
world he once revelled in was also the world where the wrong became
so strong it overcame him.

It's hard not to ponder the words of his third verse; this is indeed
our Father's world, though it has been invaded by sin and death. It is
a world where wrong is very strong. Babcock, even while he believed
in divine Providence, was unable to draw upon his belief during his
greatest crisis. Rather than resting on the hope found in God, he gave
way to despair. We do well to not condemn him. But we also do well to
remember that the fallen world in which we live blinds the eyes with
tears of grief. While this is so, Babcock was most definitely not wrong:
this is still our Father's world.

The glorious words from the classic hymn *How Great Thou Art*
remind us that God not only created all things but that He sustains all
things as well. At each moment, everything that exists continues to exist
in its present form because the Maker has willed that it should be so.

---

[9] Ibid
[10] Ibid

God rules over our messy world?

The idea of divine Providence breaks down for many of us when we ask, how do I account for disease, pain and death? The answer is that these are not the designs of the Creator, they are evidence of war against the Creator's designs. And yet, even while sin has invaded creation, the Creator continues to sustain all that is. Furthermore, it would require no effort at all for the Lord to end all this sin and death, but in His eternal wisdom He has determined not to do so at present. And it is this reality we must consider.

The world of rulership and politics continues to perplex us. Why do immoral leaders wind up in charge, swaying people to their thoughts and ideas? How is this God's will? The answer, in which the Bible is abundantly clear in Romans 13:2, is that every earthly ruler who has ever wrapped him- or herself in the mantle of earthly power was placed there by God. He does not apologize; rather, He takes credit for it.

Let's rephrase this so the point won't be missed. Whenever a ruler rules, he or she does so because God has willed it. If they remain in power but for a moment, it is because God raised them up to depose them quickly and humble them. If they reign for years, or decades, they do so because God is pleased that it should be so. This latter event is cause for rejoicing when the ruler is a person of justice and compassion, but it is cause for pain and weeping when the ruler is motivated by his or her own glory and feels no compassion for those who are suffering.

Moving from kings to all people

Let's move from the sovereign will of God over kings, presidents and prime ministers to the world of individual human lives. At the time of writing, the world's population is at 8 billion people, and each one is governed by the sovereign plans of God, whether they are people of faith or denounce God, whether they seek their neighbour's good or care little for anything but their own grandeur.

David speaks to this in Psalm 139. He acknowledges that "when he sits down and when he rises up," God is thoroughly acquainted with all his ways. God knows him so well that he knows every word on his tongue, as well as every word that will be on his tongue in the future.

Almost all Christians agree with this. If we have been taught the faith, we have been taught that God knows the past, present and the future perfectly, that He is both alpha and omega, beginning and end. No future event surprises Him or causes Him to redraw His plans. How comforting it is to know that God never evaluates or judges us based on a hunch or rumour. God is perfectly familiar with all our ways. Nothing is hidden from His sight. All is exposed. We need not attempt to deceive God, for such a thing is not possible. He knows us far more than we know ourselves, and His dealings with us are not general but specific. His knowledge of us is not second-hand but based on firsthand knowledge.

But what are we to make of Psalm 139:16? There, David says, "Your eyes saw my unformed substance . . . the days that were formed for me, when as yet there was none of them."

What it's telling us is that God not only knew us while we were in the wombs of our mothers, but that He also knew before we were born what would occur in each day of our lives on this earth. Similarly, what do we make of Job 14:5?

> Since his days are determined, and the number of his
> months is with you, and you have appointed his limits
> that he cannot pass.

Job is commenting on the length of every human life, as well as accomplishments during that time and limits on what a human will be able to do or not do. Perhaps one will be a talented pianist but will never achieve a world stage because of family commitments. All these things are in God's control and happen at His pleasure. We are again reminded to resolutely abandon the use of the term "luck," which refers to random chance events. Such a thing has not occurred to the 8 billion people on the planet. Rather, every human being has the same experience. They have encountered the determined plan of God. God has appointed both their limits and their accomplishments.

Jeremiah 10:23 says, "I know, O LORD, that the way of man is not in himself, that it is not in man who walks to direct his steps."

Proverbs 20:24 further says, "A man's steps are from the LORD; how then can man understand his way?"

We may not understand the reason for our decisions, or the way in which our lives take shape. But God understands completely because He directed each of our steps. This is good news for those who submit to God. They pray, "Oh Lord, I might plan my ways, but you direct my steps," and this belief in His Providence allows them to live without the grief of what might have been. What relief it is from bondage when one can gladly say that we would change nothing in our pasts except our sins. Furthermore, what a joy to know that even the consequences for our confessed sins work together for our eternal joy and God's glory.

But what of those who have no interest in God's ways? When the Bible says that the way of man is not in himself, it refers to all of humanity. Your destiny is not in yourself. The trajectory of your life is not in yourself. God directs your steps.

Some object. There are usually two arguments directed against the idea that each step a man or woman takes is ordered by God. The first objection is of free will. Let's be clear: our free will and choices are not illusory. They are real. God is not deceiving us, making it appear that we have freedom to choose, all the while pulling our strings as if we are puppets. Instead we are created in the image of God, with the power of choice. Furthermore, God holds us accountable for our choices precisely because they were freely made. However we understand the nature of human freedom and choices, it must be understood within the context of God's free choices, which supersede all choices. More will be said about this in later chapters. However we understand human freedom it can't be understood to contradict God's meticulous sovereignty of all things.

The second argument against the view that all human steps are ordered by God is that this will ultimately lead to fatalism. Once we adopt a view of fatalism our choices are insignificant and meaningless. Fatalism always leads to indifference. Human choices don't matter. Hence wisdom and moral choices are also meaningless. If God orders our steps, are we not left with fatalism? My answer is that we are not.

We must consider this matter at length. Let us agree that no human being has *unbounded* free will—God bounds each human decision. You may wish to personally explore the far reaches of the galaxy, but God prevents you from achieving this purpose for yourself. Furthermore, you may also wish that you would never die but God overrides this. When we think about it, we will discover that so much of life is bounded. You may freely decide to be a brilliant physicist but be limited by an average IQ. You may wish to gain a PhD in computer science but be born in a third-world country village with no access to even a modest education, let alone electricity. You may decide you want to play centre for an NBA team, but if you are 5'7" you will not succeed.

So much of our free will is bounded by countless realities, and this has always been the case, for every human being. In my early years I had thought I would be a singer-songwriter, but my talents proved insufficient for the task. Instead I have spent my life bringing people to Jesus, which is God's plan for me, and a good one at that.

North Americans love this familiar mantra: you can become anything you want to be if you are willing to pay the price to get it. But is it true? What if you contract an incurable disease tomorrow? What if you don't have the academic credentials to get into Harvard or Princeton? What if you are 5'7" and want to play basketball in the NBA? These are things that, regardless of the effort, you will not achieve.

We are limited. We are bounded by God. A multiplicity of factors defined by him both limit and enhance us. These factors influence our life paths and our decision-making processes. They include economic advantage, health, IQ, where and when we were born, the country of our birth, the family that raised us and, last but not least, timing. As the saying goes, timing is everything. A decision made at the right stage of life, at the right time in history, can lead to wild success. Not being in the right place at the right time can lead one down the opposite path.

We all enjoy stories of people who have overcome great obstacles in life to achieve goals or various versions of success but these, just like tales of great tragedy, are still controlled by God. Proverbs 16:9 tells us: "The heart of man plans his way, but the Lord establishes his steps."

In other words, life is what happens while we were making other plans.

My story

Compare my personal testimony to your own story. I unexpectedly came to faith in Christ at the age of eighteen. Prior to that, if you had asked me how my life was going to work out I would have said I was either going to take over my parents' dairy farm or enter business. Furthermore, I was going to write music. I was not averse to marriage but thought I should delay it as long as possible. After all, nothing, but *nothing*, should get in the way of pursuing my desires and dreams.

I surrendered to the grace that came through the cross of Jesus at the age of eighteen. At that time I was still planning my own way. But I had a fear: what if God's plan for my life involved something I did not want? So a part of my conversion prayer included a request. I asked God never to call me into full-time Christian work. Most specifically, I did not wish to be a pastor. The reason for this request was not that I did not admire some pastors I knew. There were several pastors whom I greatly admired. But I liked fast cars and motorcycles. All the pastors I knew drove sensible sedans and station wagons. Furthermore, congregations found the cars I like to be unacceptable. And the idea of being governed in non-moral issues by the sensibilities of others struck me as oppressive. I did not wish to become a man who constantly asked what others thought.

As a young man, if I had been given the power to see my own future and where my life would take me I would have been shocked. God had plans for me that I could not even imagine, and they were so much different from my own (except I do own a motorcycle). My way was hemmed in by God. He determined my steps. He appointed the limits I was not allowed to cross. When I was being formed in my mother's womb, he had already directed the footsteps of my life. Had I chosen for myself, I would have chosen rebellion to his purposes. But I was delivered up to the light of God's glorious presence! Not *my* will be done, but *His*.

Your story, too

According to the Bible, my life's story is true of all those who are saved by grace. In Galatians 1:15, Paul says, "But when He who had set me apart before I was born, and who called me by His grace." And God said to Jeremiah in Jeremiah 1:5, "Before I formed you in the womb I knew you, and before you were born, I consecrated you; I appointed you a prophet to the nations."

Yes, Christians can and must see the pre-determining hand of God in their lives. We are required to revel in the one who "chose us in him before the foundation of the world" (Ephesians 1:4).

In Psalm 139 we learned that God determined our ways while we were being formed in our mother's womb, but in Ephesians (above) we learn this occurred before the world was even born! And that is the source of joy. What grace! What glory must go to God! Rather than viewing this as a source of frustration and the loss of our vision for our lives, we must view this as the source of joy. Our wills have been defeated! God's will has prevailed!

But is the will of God realized in all lives?

Does God's will rule the lives of all people? Is God's will done in the lives of those who don't believe, or those who actively resist his will? Earlier I mentioned Mick Jagger, who sang, "You can't always get what you want." Does God always get what He wants? Or is His will thwarted by the billions who refuse to bend the knee to Him? Is humanity's story about human will triumphing over God's? Could God be defeated by the choices of those who refuse His grace?

The battle between human will and the will of God is an ongoing biblical theme. We must, however, not be in doubt about the outcome of this contest. Furthermore, while the Bible might not answer *all* our questions about the nature of God and man, it answers more questions than we might realize. The testimony of scripture is that it depends not on human will or exertion, but on God who has mercy.

God's choice and human choices

The debate about how God rules human lives tends to be intense, and yet, as we have seen, the Bible makes it clear that God directs the course of each human life. God chooses and so do we—but what happens when our choice and His oppose each other?

As I mentioned before, our power of choice is not imaginary. It is real. And it is because we have real choices that the Bible commands us to choose. Deuteronomy 30:19 records Moses preaching evangelistically to Israel. He says:

> I call Heaven and earth to witness against you today, that I have set before you life and death, blessing and curse. Therefore, choose life, that you and your offspring may live, loving the LORD your God, obeying his voice and holding fast to him.

Joshua's evangelistic sermon to Israel in Joshua 24:15 says:

> And if it is evil in your eyes to serve the LORD, choose this day whom you will serve, whether the gods your fathers served in the region beyond the River, or the gods of the Amorites in whose land you dwell. But as for me and my house, we will serve the LORD.

My wife Kathy and I have engraved in our marriage rings the words of Micah 4:5:

> For all the peoples walk each in the name of its god, but we will walk in the name of the LORD our God forever and ever.

That verse reminds us that human beings have all made choices about the gods they will serve. They might be the ancient gods of wood and stone or the modern gods of wealth and technology. Whatever they are, the gods people choose to worship represent who or what they love. We worship that which we believe to be *ultimate*. These are the things that dominate our affections. People make choices in this regard all the time. Kathy and I have made our choice, and we engraved it on our rings to proclaim that we walk in the name of the Lord, regardless of what the rest of the world chooses to do.

There are consequences for the real choices we all make. The God of the Bible holds us to account for our decisions and we cannot deny it. However, it is at this very point that we often fall into a mental trap. Since we are commanded to choose, we then assume that our power of choice and not God's governs our lives. We do well then to question our thinking. Who ultimately rules, and whose choices ultimately matter? Are our choices so significant that God is placed into the role of being a responder to our choices, or is the opposite true? Which choices control the future?

Many inadvertently come to worship their own choices. Hence they assume when their lot in life is better than someone else's, it is due to making good and profitable choices. This leads to arrogance. After all, if their choices determine the future, the success they experience in their life is assumed to have come from their superior decisions rather than the permission of God. All of this leads to a lack of compassion for those who fail and a sense of the superiority in those who succeed.

Psalm 75:6–7 says:

> For not from the east or from the west and not from the wilderness comes lifting up, but it is God who executes judgment, putting down one and lifting up another.

Think of that. When one is lifted (brought to prominence) and another is put down (removed from prominence) it is the work of God.

A little thought tells us this must be so. I have read accounts of some of the great computer geniuses—Bill Gates, Steve Jobs, and others—who shaped the modern computer era. These gifted and motivated men came to prominence because they were born at the right time, were in the right place and were given the right opportunities. Take away the factors they did not control and the world would never have heard of them. The time, place and opportunities were in the hands of God.

Mary, the mother of Jesus, said that very thing. Luke 1:52 records her as saying, "He has brought down the mighty from their thrones and exalted those of humble estate."

She said exactly what was said in Psalm 75: "He lifts one and puts down another."

We generally think it unfair that some people receive opportunities that we don't. Sometimes we complain that, had we been given such opportunities, we too could have done well. But it does no good to live in envy. We must never forget that God grants or withholds opportunity at his will. God and not our choices rules this world and the kingdoms of men.

But there is more. The power of each individual intellect is controlled by God. So are our unique talents and natural abilities. Paul said so in 1 Corinthians 4:7. He asks, "What do you have that you did not receive? If then you received it, why do you boast as if you did not receive it?"

In this passage, Paul mounts a full-frontal assault on human pride. Fallen human reasoning loves the idea of the self-made man or woman. But that idea is an illusion. With a single breath God can change all and turn anyone's life on its ear.

I am not belittling the power of choice. I am, however, reminding us that choices happen in a context. Children born in poverty in Bangladesh will likely never become the next Warren Buffet. They will have limited access to education, and may never know the wonders of advanced science, for example. Of course, there are notable exceptions. There are amazing stories of people growing up in poverty and in conditions that make success seem unattainable. There is something about the image of God in all people that speaks of human courage to conquer against all odds. We should revel in this reality, for the human spirit can rise above the most abhorrent disadvantages. But even in these stories of great human courage, God controls all the things that give us opportunity, including our intellect, drive, opportunities, looks, health and even the friends who either push us forward or hold us back. It is all controlled by God.

David, when talking about his military skill, said God had equipped him with strength. In Psalm 18:33-34, he said, "He made my feet like the feet of a deer and set me secure on the heights. He trains my hands for war, so that my arms can bend a bow of bronze."

David is saying, "Look, this is the reason I was so successful in battle. I have great physical strength. I have an incredible sense of balance. I have confidence in the day of battle. God made me that way."

Furthermore, decisions rulers make are also made under God's care. Proverbs 21:1 says, "The king's heart is a stream of water in the hand of the LORD; he turns it wherever he will."

God oversees political rulers, every aspect of their dominion and every decision they make. Change but a few factors in their reign and they would have a very different outcome.

How does God rule our free choices?

How does God control all things, including our free choices? Think about Babylon's King Nebuchadnezzar. God subjected him to countless miracles others were not privy to. God also drove him into madness until he acknowledged that the God of heaven rules. It's an amazing account of how God manipulated a pagan king.

Think also of Cyrus, king of Persia. Long before Cyrus was born, God spoke to Jeremiah the prophet. God told Jeremiah that Israel would go into captivity for her sin, and that after they had been in captivity for seventy years He would bring them to the Promised Land.

Ezra 1:1 says:

> In the first year of Cyrus king of Persia, that the word of the Lord by the mouth of Jeremiah might be fulfilled, the Lord stirred up the spirit of Cyrus king of Persia, so that he made a proclamation throughout all his kingdom and also put it in writing.

Jeremiah 29:10 says:

> For thus says the LORD: When seventy years are completed for Babylon, I will visit you, and I will fulfill to you my promise and bring you back to this place.

Imagine the scenario: God caused Nebuchadnezzar of Babylon to attack Israel, burn its temple down and drag the nation into exile, and then, after seventy years of exile, he caused Cyrus of Persia to issue a decree to bring them back. Both were pagan kings making free choices, yet their choices were directed by God. God had already planned the role they would play long before they were even born!

God directs the footsteps of every human, from king to peasant. He determines the opportunities encountered, the skill and talent they bring to those opportunities, everything required to bring any given situation to fruition under God. God manages the whole universe and every atom it contains.

But how does He do this? This study still lies before us; however, scripture has a great deal to say. Psalm 33:13-15:

> The LORD looks down from Heaven; he sees all the children of man; from where he sits enthroned, he looks out on all the inhabitants of the earth, he who fashions the hearts of them all.

In the early part of that Psalm we are told that God not only created all things, but that He also directs them. Verse 7 says that He puts the deeps into storehouses, while verse 10 says the Lord brings the counsel of nations to nothing, and that He frustrates the plans of peoples. What this means is that every occurrence in the universe is at his discretion alone. After verse 15, the psalmist tells us that a king is not saved by his army, a warrior is not saved by his mighty strength and a war horse does not guarantee success in battle. Why? Because God frustrates human plans and determines what will come to pass.

Maltbie Babcock was correct when he said, "Though the wrong seems oft so strong, God is the Ruler yet." If only Pastor Babcock had reminded himself of that when his body was wracked with pain and his spirit was sinking into depression. But that is the truth: God is the ruler yet. He created all things. He holds all things together. He ensures that all things that occur on earth are according to the purpose of His will. He directs the course of every nation and He directs the trajectory of every human life.

Christians rest assured that human will can never override the plans and intentions of God. God rules! Human will and human power do not. What comforting words!

CHAPTER 6

God Rules Over Good and Evil

Are you bothered by evil? Do you sometimes cry out to God because of it? Are you disheartened when evil people triumph, live in peace and prosper? Does the plight of their victims fill your heart with anger? Are you astonished by the pride evil people wear, as if it were an expensive piece of jewelry to be displayed? Does it shock you that they have no fear of God? Does it perplex you that it appears that God does not lift a finger against them? Are you bothered by evil? If you are not, you should be.

The psalmist Asaph said that evil people scoff and speak with malice while they loftily threaten to oppress all opposition. He said the mouths of evil people speak against heaven itself. They curse God and His Son Jesus without even the slightest twinge of fear. And their tongues strut through the earth like the chief rooster among the chickens.

Here is a list of some of the things in this world that sometimes plague my spirit. I am bothered by the persecution of Christians and the rising tide of intolerance towards Christians. I am bothered by resistance to the truth of Jesus. I am grieved by the entrenched atheism of the Western world. I am deeply disturbed by the practice of aborting unborn children. I find the worldwide refugee crisis disturbing, men, women and children uprooted from their homes and forced to flee all over the world. I am disturbed by brutal violence that occurs when countries invade other countries and the civilians who are raped, tortured and killed. Furthermore, I grieve when I hear of mass shootings, which seem to be occurring more and more frequently. I also grieve when I see the homelessness in my own country, one of the wealthiest nations in the history of humanity.

I find my heart does not bear this world lightly. I also know that Jesus, my Saviour, told me that the regenerate hearts of the redeemed are meant to be grieved. Yes, we are grieved by sin because we are longing for God's ways and God's blessings. Jesus said, "Blessed are those who hunger and thirst for righteousness, for they shall be satisfied" (Matthew 5:6).

Jesus said we are to do more than be grieved by evil. We are to anticipate the day when righteousness prevails, just as a starving man anticipates the moment that he will have food. That, said Jesus, blesses those who await the sunset of evil and the dawn of righteousness. But it is not easy, and it can be all-consuming. I have spoken to people who have suffered hunger. They tell me that dreams of food interrupt their sleep. Likewise, dreams of a just world can do the same.

Thus, those who think that Christians, with their faith in a sovereign, meticulous God who always gets what He wants, are unconcerned over evil have it wrong. Instead, our belief in God inflames a passion to see the end of evil days.

Until now, when discussing evil and sin I have only spoken about big things, meaning things *many* people notice, like the workings of governments and nations or natural disasters; however, there are many small things that occur every day that can wreck the lives of men and women and are only relevant to the people involved. Examples include people taking advantage of each other, or slandering others, or abusing power in the workplace or home. Consequences of this behaviour can be someone losing their job or reputation, lawsuits that drag on and drain bank accounts and so on.

When this type of evil occurs, it seems to those experiencing it that justice is a privilege only for those who can afford it. Christians, if they are *truly* Christians, take these forms of evil seriously. We believe God has called us to be our "brother's keeper" and that we should proclaim our loyalty to Christ by working for the justice of the oppressed. Sexual trafficking, sexual abuse and sexual slavery, especially of children, is particularly diabolical, and many Christian organizations are on the front lines in countries around the world, working to end this practice.

Evil, which resulted from the original fall of Adam, is so pervasive that if we allowed ourselves to think of the suffering that arises from this earth every day we would all have difficulty sleeping. To manage our way through this world of evil, most of us either blind our eyes or harden our hearts. Who can remain constantly sensitive to evil?

Only one could do that. Jesus is different from the rest of us. During His human life He was completely aware of evil. He saw it, felt it and resisted it at every turn. This world, and the evil that is rampant on it, could not tolerate the Son of God. We nailed him to a cross.

When I pray about such things, I worry that it sometimes borders on blasphemy. "Why, O God, do you tolerate and allow such evil to continue?" I ask the Lord. "Is it that you just don't care? I know you have wider purposes, but why do you look upon the suffering of so many and not act? Are You passively watching as so many of your children die in misery? Are you not acting because you are angry with us beyond measure? Are you hiding your face from our wretchedness?"

Nevertheless, I do not lose hope. The promises God has made regarding the coming of his eternal Kingdom are not vain promises. And if God has determined that the world we presently experience will see a foretaste of both heaven and hell, I will rest in his wisdom. I am also convinced that the existence of evil will manifest itself whether we will fight for righteousness as we are able, or whether we will merely acquiesce. It takes courage to fight. It takes no courage to ignore.

The easy answers

I am aware that some reading these lines will condemn me for praying as I do. What right do I have to challenge the eternal wisdom of God? And I agree. But the presence of evil should create a deep sense of unease in all of us. Furthermore, the easy answer, that evil exists because God allows people to exercise their free will, is unacceptable.

We have become accustomed to the free-will argument when it comes to abortion. "Men and women have the freedom to choose," we say. But this argument is unsatisfactory. What free will did the unborn child have who was deprived of that most precious of all gifts, the gift of life? And what of the free will of the refugee, the orphan and the one who lives in crushing, unremitting poverty? I find the easy free-will answers to the problem of evil tragically naive. Perhaps the easy answers allow us to gain relief from the problem of evil. People choose evil, we say. But the easy answers also betray our lack of compassion: it neglects to examine how evil is practiced against those who have no free will at all.

The harder questions

Instead of resorting to easy answers, perhaps we should ask harder questions. Of course we do wrong to blame God for evil. Deuteronomy 32:4 reminds us of the character of God: "The Rock, his work is perfect, for all his ways are justice. A God of faithfulness and without iniquity, just and upright is he."

God does no wrong. Our hands are unclean, but he does all things well. 1 John 1:5 proudly proclaims, "This is the message we have heard from him and proclaim to you, that God is light, and in him is no darkness at all."

As Christians we are required to acknowledge the just character of God, and yet scripture itself demands that we ask hard questions about iniquity. Habakkuk 1:3 says, "Why do you make me see iniquity, and why do you idly look at wrong?"

That's the hard question, but questions and lament are part of a believer's burden, and honest cries to God are a necessary part of relationship with him. He wants us to look at iniquity (injustice and deceit) and wrong (suffering). Not to do so demonstrates unconcern for others and their welfare.

There are many occasions when evil continues without a stop sign from heaven. It is undoubtedly true that any evil would have been greater than it is were it not for the restraining hand of God. Nonetheless, what has occurred has come about because the righteous God of heaven has willed that it should not be restrained. We need to ask why this is so. That's the harder question.

Our questions of evil must be asked on the foundation we have laid

Our study has led us to the point that we can and must affirm that God is the author of all the created order, both the visible and invisible. All that exists has come into being because He called it. Furthermore, all that exists continues to exist at each moment because the righteous Creator wills that it should. We have also found this to be true in the inanimate world and in the world of all living things.

As we discussed earlier, God is immediately involved in all things. Remember the story of the ostrich? God had a purpose in making the ostrich exactly the way it is. God makes all things to serve His purposes, including things that reflect wisdom and foolishness. God places earth's natural features, directs the weather, manages the affairs of nations and creates the paths for each human being.

The Bible, the meticulously sovereign God and evil

God's meticulous rule gives us confidence and joy, but if His kind and good providence rules all things, how is it that he sustains evil? The Bible speaks to this matter explicitly. As we examine biblical teaching we may be discomfited by what we find. Easy answers are shattered. A different picture than what many expect takes shape. Let's start with Genesis 50:20. Joseph's deceitful brothers sold him into slavery, and God did not appear to have intervened.

This was an evil act. But what actually happened? As we examine the passage, we find that God was constantly intervening. Joseph rose to great prominence in the house of a wealthy and powerful Egyptian lord. This would not have occurred if God had prevented the evil of his brothers selling him into slavery. What happened next? A duplicitous woman defamed him and he was sent to jail. For a time he languished in prison, until God rescued him. Eventually, Joseph rose to become the second most powerful man in Egypt and went on to not only save his family from starvation during a famine, but many others as well, and all of it started with an evil act committed by his brothers under the direction of God. But then came the last bit of business. Joseph would still need to deal with the wickedness of his brothers.

We see that Joseph was able to forgive his brothers. He did so with an eye to the greater purpose of God. He said to them, "You intended it for evil, but God intended it for good" (Genesis 50:20).

Joseph believed the act of enslaving him was inherently evil but that God intended it. God refused to step in to prevent his brothers from acting out of jealousy, the slave traders from buying him, Potiphar from purchasing him as a slave and his duplicitous wife from slandering him. All these were evil acts, done with evil intent. But Joseph also believed that God intended that this act should be allowed to go ahead. There would be no stop sign along the way.

What shall we then conclude? It must be this: *Intent is everything!* Imagine a young man tackling an elderly woman on the street. She is bruised and psychologically shaken. What should we make of such a thing? That depends on intent. If he tackled her to steal her purse, the act was evil. But if he tackled her because he saw that she was in the way of a speeding car and saved her life, then it was a righteous act. Even though in both cases she was tackled, bruised and psychologically shaken, intent made the difference. And it is the same with what happened to Joseph. While Joseph's brothers' intent was evil when they sold him into slavery, God's intent was that Joseph would save a multitude of lives. We must then conclude that while, in this present dispensation, God allows evil to exist, his intent in doing so is the deciding factor. No, it is not the evil. It is the intent.

Let's move to another text. In Exodus 4:21, we are told that God hardened Pharaoh's heart when Moses demanded Pharaoh release God's chosen people from unjust slavery. Pharaoh refused because the slaves were valuable to the economy; furthermore, to acquiesce to Moses would have shown weakness in his authority. Ultimately, because Pharaoh did not listen to Moses, God rained ten plagues onto Egypt and suffering ensued. This suffering was a horrible thing, but it also proclaimed the glory of God to Israel and the rest of the Middle East. Had Pharaoh let Israel go, the Red Sea would not have parted and Israel would not have stood in awe of the majesty of God who rescued them. Had God not hardened Pharaoh's heart, the Lord's power, compassion and glory would have remained hidden. God's intent was that the earth should know Him.

Let's move on to the book of Joshua. Joshua 11:20 speaks of the nations in Canaan, saying, "For it was the LORD's doing to harden their hearts that they should come against Israel in battle, in order that they should be devoted to destruction and should receive no mercy."

The reason so many nations in Canaan were destroyed in battle was because God ruled the hearts of those people to act in ways that would reduce them to destruction—God determined that it be so. In this way, God made it known that His ways are not to be rejected. That was God's intent.

In Judges 3:12, we are told that, "The LORD strengthened Eglon the king of Moab against Israel."

The reason? God was determined to punish Israel for her idolatry and to ensure Israel faced consequences for abandoning him. God also strengthened the evil Moabite king, Eglon, so this wicked man gained power because God willed it. In the end, however, Eglon was destroyed and God revealed that he will destroy all wicked men. When God destroyed Eglon, Israel was reminded to put hope only in God. That was God's intent.

Here's another example. In Judges 14:4, we read about Samson being interested in a Philistine woman. Samson was determined to be with this woman, either to marry her or have her as his concubine. Not only did this upset his parents, but it was in direct violation of the law of God. Deuteronomy 7:3–4 says:

> You shall not intermarry with them, giving your daughters to their sons or taking their daughters for your sons, for they would turn away your sons from following me, to serve other gods. Then the anger of the LORD would be kindled against you, and he would destroy you quickly.

What Samson was about to do was a wicked thing and a violation of God's law. Samson was planning to sin against God. And he did it. He married the woman. Why? He was motivated by lust and attracted to that which was forbidden. But just when we think we understand all there is to be understood, the scripture surprises us. Judges 14:4 tells us:

"His father and mother did not know that it was from the LORD, for he was seeking an opportunity against the Philistines."

Translation: Samson's illegal marriage was from God. God intended to use this incident to cause harm to the Philistines, the enemies of God. That was the difference between Sampson's intent, and God's intent.

We come now to 1 Samuel 2:25. This passage talks about the sons of Eli the priest who had no regard for the ways of God and determined to use sacrifices to him for their own wealth and benefit. Verse 25 says, "But they would not listen to the voice of their father, for it was the will of the LORD to put them to death."

The sons of Eli refused to treat the sacrificial offering as a holy thing. Their intent was to sin against God and become wealthy in the process. In other words, these young men were hardened to righteousness because God had already determined they would die in their sins. God arranged matters in this fashion to declare that sacrifices to God would be treated as *holy*. That was God's intent.

There is more evidence of this. In 2 Samuel 12, in which David is told that God will punish him for murdering Uriah and sleeping with his wife, verse 11 says:

> This is what the LORD says, "Out of your own household I am going to bring calamity on you. Before your very eyes I will take your wives and give them to one who is close to you."

How can God say, "I will bring calamity on you?" Isn't it the devil who raises up disasters or adversities? Or the free choice of humans who are sinners by nature? And yet, scripture says God Himself can raise up trouble at His discretion. In this case, He does so to teach David and all future kings that kingship is not license to use power in an unbridled way. This was God's intent.

There are two passages in scripture that at first brush seem contradictory. One passage is in 2 Samuel. The other occurs in 1 Chronicles. Both describe the same event. David has sinned when conducting a census of Israel. God is not pleased. 2 Samuel 24:1 says,

"Again, the anger of the LORD was kindled against Israel, and he incited David against them, saying, 'Go, number Israel and Judah.'"

From the perspective of 2 Samuel, Israel's sin was the first cause of what was to come. And then, following the unrepentant sin of the nation, God incited David to take an illegal census. That in itself might seem perplexing. How can God incite sin? But we must not think that David sinned against his own will. Rather, we must think that David willed to sin, and that God willed not to intervene and stop him. It was all about intent.

The parallel account of this incident is found in 1 Chronicles 21:1: "Then Satan stood against Israel and incited David to number Israel."

Do you see the difficulty? 2 Samuel says that it was God who caused David to sin, while 1 Chronicles says it was Satan who did this. Was it God or Satan who caused this?

The answer is that it was both. Recall Martin Luther's statement that the devil is none other than the unwilling servant of God. Satan's rebellion plays right into the intent and purpose of God and, as much as Satan hates and despises him, he cannot help but serve him. In that context, Satan's involvement is no different than the involvement of Joseph's brothers in his enslavement: Satan intended evil while God intended a showcase of his righteousness.

And so we come to an important conclusion about evil: it seeks to resist God at every step, but serves God at every step because God is ruler of all. Does it sound strange that evil serves God? If this is true, does this make God culpable in evil? Furthermore, did God *create* evil? And if he did, does He sustain it, moment by moment, as he sustains all other things? Does that mean God uses evil design to accomplish His purposes? If that were the case, the entire nature of our faith would lie in ruins. God would be charged with evil, and we would have no basis for trusting in him.

But God is not to be charged with evil. 1 John 1:5 is clear on this: "God is light, and in Him, there is no darkness at all."

James 1:13 says, "Let no one say when he is tempted, 'I am being tempted by God,' for God cannot be tempted with evil, and he himself tempts no one."

Scripture is plain: God never acts out of dark or evil intent and God never entices people to act in evil ways. God is not the author of evil. God does not delight in wickedness. God never rejoices in that which is impure. And yet God rules over evil, for He rules over all things.

The natural question, then, is "how can evil exist?" For if God is Creator of all, must He then have created evil? The resounding answer from Scripture is no! But then, how are we to understand the existence of evil? While the Bible does not directly answer this question, Augustine, the great Christian teacher, had a good explanation. He taught that evil is not a thing; rather, he said, it is the *absence* of a thing.[11] It is the absence of God's goodness and righteousness. Hence, rebellion against God is the absence of willing submission to God. Even though there is in many places the absence of submission to God, God rules over such absence. God is not the author of evil, but He rules it utterly.

There is shock among believers when they are introduced to what the Bible says about God's rule over evil for the first time.

- In 1 Kings 11:14: "The Lord raised up an adversary against Solomon." That is, an evil man was raised up by God.
- In Job 1:22: "The LORD gave, and the LORD has taken away."
- In 1 Kings 22:23: "The LORD has put a lying spirit in the mouths of the false prophets." The lying spirit was already there. God did not create the lie. But God determined that the lying, evil spirit should inhabit the mouths of the false prophets.

Examples fill the pages of scripture, and the fact that many Christians have not been trained to pay attention to these passages is a tragedy because it means we misunderstand God's dealings in the world.

Two more important scriptures

I want us to examine two more passages of scripture. They come to us from two Old Testament prophets. The first is Amos. Amos 3:6 reads: "Is

---

[11]   Augustine. *Confessions*. Grand Rapids, MI: Christian Classics Ethereal Library, n.d.

a trumpet blown in a city, and the people are not afraid? Does disaster come to a city, unless the LORD has done it?"

Amos couldn't be clearer. When a trumpet sounds and signals the attack of an army, God is the author of that disaster. The Lord has done it, says Amos.

I know that many rage against this thought and say, "God has nothing to do with tragedy. It is the devil. It is nature gone awry. It is wicked people." But scripture says the opposite. God has everything to do with everything. He sustains all things. Furthermore, God is not embarrassed by the evil in the world; instead, God proclaims that nothing, not even evil itself, can carry on for a moment if not for His providential hand. It is time we stop hearing the misinformed line that God had nothing to do with it.

Here is one more passage from the Old Testament to consider. Isaiah 45:7 says, "I form light and create darkness; I make well-being and create calamity; I am the LORD, who does all these things."

The word that is translated as "calamity" is the Hebrew word "ra," which is often translated as "evil"—two possible ways of translating the same word. We have the same range of meaning in the English language. "Evil" can mean different things. The word can be used in a moral sense, such as rebellion against God's laws and his righteous character. But the word can also be used in terms of the consequences of an event. In this second sense, we may say, "Great evil has resulted from this calamity," in the wake of earthquakes, floods and other disasters.

In Isaiah, "evil" is described as calamity, not moral rebellion. The evil Isiah speaks of is *consequence*, in this case is an invading foreign army. God says, "I did it. I created the calamity. It came from my hand. Make no mistake about it. I control everything that occurs in this world."

Getting back to our questions

By now it should be apparent that the easy questions and answers have no place in this discussion. And even though we can't answer all the weighty questions, we can allow the Bible to answer the main one: "Why does God permit evil?" In some mysterious fashion, God will cause all the evil that occurs in the world to result in the best of possible outcomes. Those outcomes will be for the glory of God and the eternal good of His chosen people.

Let's consider one of the great prayers in the Bible, prayed by the early church after Peter and John were arrested and thrown into prison for teaching and preaching that Jesus had been raised from the dead. You can imagine the anxiety among Jesus's early flock: his two successors—the two most prominent leaders of the early church—had been arrested. What if they were executed? What would happen to the infant Christian movement? Then, in marvelous mercy, the two men were released, and so those early Christians did what all Christians have done since then: they called a church-wide prayer meeting to thank God for his mercy in securing the release of their leaders.

Acts 4:27–28:

> For truly in this city there were gathered together against your holy servant Jesus, whom you anointed, both Herod and Pontius Pilate, along with the Gentiles and the peoples of Israel, to do whatever your hand and your plan had predestined to take place.

What gave the early Church such strength and confidence? It was their unshakeable faith in divine Providence. Basically, the prayer above says, "We understand that you predestined the crucifixion of Jesus so that the most lovely thing could occur. Jesus died for the sins of His people! He opened wide a door for the salvation of many. What was intended by wicked men to be an evil act was intended by God for goodness and salvation. We know that if you can rule over the evil crucifixion of your Son, Jesus, you will also rule over the arrest of Peter and John and it will be to maximize your glory and the good of your people."

From that paradigm came the confidence the early Church needed. Through the crucifixion they had come to believe that even evil itself was being used by God for greater and better purposes. Evil, which is still evil, is not authored by God. But evil is under God's providential hand.

Conclusion

Who then is responsible for evil? We have already confirmed that it is not God, for He is never the author of evil. Instead, evildoers are responsible for their own evil. The crucifixion of Christ, although predestined, was still evil. And yet Peter said that the crucifixion of Jesus was foreknown before the foundation of the earth itself (1 Peter 1:20). Even so, it was carried out by wicked men, and those wicked men were held to account by God for crucifying the Lord of glory.

Let's be clear: the crucifixion of the Son of God was the most astonishingly evil act done since the creation of the world. No evil enacted on humans—be it ethnic cleansing, the aborting of unborn children or concentration camps where heinous crime occurs—comes close to the evil that was done when, at the hands of wicked men, the perfect Son of God was nailed to a cross.

But much good came out of that evil. The resurrection of Jesus gave the early Church courage to continue spreading his message of reconciliation between God and man. It laid the foundation for the Christian movement. And it should give *us* courage as well. As Christians, we don't know how God will bring good out of every evil situation, but we must have faith that He is doing so. When horrible things happen we need to imagine how they will serve the good. Deuteronomy 29:29 says that "secret things" belong to the Lord and are part of his mysterious purpose. At times, the good that will yet come out of evil is one of God's secret things.

As Christians, we know that we are not to be evil; in fact, we are required to be peacemakers and to work to end injustice. It is God's command. According to Romans 13:3, God appointed rulers and government to bring about laws to terrorize evil and protect would-be victims. British slavery abolitionist William Wilberforce, a Member of Parliament from 31 October 1780 to February 1825, when campaigning against the practice of slavery in England, would never have said, "If God rules over evil, I should do nothing." Instead, he worked tirelessly to make slavery obsolete.

In the same vein, if we are personally wronged we should seek legal justice. However, we shouldn't be surprised to discover that God permitted evil to occur against us to test what was in our hearts. God had a vested interest in knowing whether we will make peace with it or fight relentlessly against it. The presence of suffering in this world demands of every believer that we become the agents of righteousness and that wickedness becomes our enemy. Furthermore, it demands that we show love and mercy rather than indifference. And we must never make peace with evil. If we do not fight evil, we *become* evil.

Lamentations 3:38 says: "Is it not from the mouth of the Most High that good and bad come?"

And since everything comes from the mouth of God, we will not fear, for even though the wrong seems so strong, God is the ruler yet.

Concluding thought

The English writer Somerset Maugham once wrote a story about a janitor at St. Peter's Church in London. One day a young vicar discovered that the janitor was illiterate and he fired him. Jobless, the man invested his miserably small savings in a tiny tobacco shop, where he prospered. He bought another shop, expanded and eventually ended up with a chain of tobacco stores worth several hundred thousand dollars.

One day the man's banker said, "You've done well for an illiterate man, but where would you be if you could read and write?"

"Well," replied the man, "I'd be janitor of St. Peter's Church in Neville Square."

The same could be said of Joseph, the prime minister of Egypt. What if he had never been sold into slavery? It would have resulted in the starvation of many and Joseph would never have saved a multitude of people from starvation. Hence, we should not fear. God does all things for His glory and our long-term good.

CHAPTER 7

Two Wills in God

A great many people have two different wills. They want something, but they also want something else. This may carry on without incident for some time, but eventually the two competing desires clash and one must give way to the other. In the Bible, Jesus spoke of this when He said that we cannot serve both God and money. James also mentions it when he says a double-minded man is unstable in all his ways.

Imagine a person who both wants to be famous *and* humble. Those two desires can't coexist because, while it is possible to be both famous and humble, it is not possible to *desire* being both famous and humble. If fame is a goal, then humility must be forsaken.

Here are some examples of some humble people who inadvertently became famous:

- Florence Nightingale. She went to the Crimean War to nurse wounded soldiers and saved countless wounded men using methods she'd developed that were so far ahead of her time that she paved the way for modern nursing. She became famous not because she was *seeking* fame, but because she was motivated by a desire to save suffering soldiers.
- Frederick Banting, a Canadian medical scientist, discovered insulin. As with Nightingale, he was pursuing something quite unrelated to fame.
- William Wilberforce, whom I mentioned earlier, led the charge to end slavery in England.

In each of these cases, fame was a *biproduct* of heroic service on behalf of humanity, not the goal. The people we remember as virtuous are noted by their singular approach to life. Lesser goals are jettisoned to achieve a higher calling. It may be that, once having achieved fame, arrogance and pride creep in. But it is also equally possible that the person achieving fame eschews the trappings of arrogance and remains humble. Fame and humility need not be contradictory. But one cannot desire both. In that case, one of the two desires will poison the other.

There are people who become famous because they have mastered the art of self-promotion and are expert at featuring themselves and their talents. These people are never humble, because humility would demand they put someone or something before themselves. The truly humble person is not concerned about accolades, but the person seeking fame must lay humble thoughts aside to achieve their goals.

But let us say that, despite this, someone is determined to seek these two goals at the same time and has convinced themselves that they can live together. They continue to pursue two wills. What occurs then? The answer is that one will is destined to utterly triumph over the other.

This was Jesus's point when He said that no one can serve both God and money. In the end, such a person will come to love one of those two better than the other. Even in the Christian Church, this can be seen. Some mega-church pastors live in unfettered luxury, with private airplanes and so on. Although they deny it, it is apparent to all that the love of money has overcome the love they once had for God. Sadly, I have known more than one pastor who has come to treat God as if He were an idol to be manipulated at will.

How can God have two wills?

What if God willed two things rather than one? Would He not be destined to the same fate? But since God is righteous and seeks His own glory, His desire is never hindered by lesser desires. How then can we consider two wills in God?

And yet it appears that God has willed that evil would continue to exist, even as He wills that evil should come to an end. This is clear because all that now exists is so because God has willed it should be.

In the case of evil, we have stated that, while God is opposed to all evil, He has for his own purposes willed that it should continue to remain for a time. But even so, God is determined that evil should come to an end. In Habakkuk 2:14, God declares his ultimate plans: "For the earth will be filled with the knowledge of the glory of the LORD as the waters cover the sea."

And yet, while God wills that justice roll down, He also wills that justice be held back for a time. We conclude that God wills the existence of evil, and He also wills that evil be vanquished with justice and righteousness. We must not conclude that God is unable to end the day of evil immediately. As we have seen, Psalm 115:3 assures us: "Our God is in the Heavens; He does all that He pleases."

We therefore affirm that whatever God wills, He does. Nothing can occur outside of His will. Furthermore, whatever God does, He does because it pleases Him to do so. The will of God always produces what God wants. And yet, Jesus taught us to pray: "Your will be done, on earth as it is in Heaven" (Matthew 6:10).

This well-known part of the Lord's Prayer indicates there is a difference in the way God's will is presently done in heaven as opposed to how it is done on earth. That is, from the time of Adam's fall into sin until the time of the restoration of all things, things on earth (in the present) are very different than things in heaven. Jesus's prayer seems to indicate that things on earth often don't function according to God's will in heaven! Indeed, we are to pray earnestly that the present state of events comes to an end, so that God's will is done on earth as it is done in heaven.

"Your will be done on earth as it is in heaven"

In Timothy 2:4, Paul says of God: "Who desires all people to be saved and to come to the knowledge of the truth."

This is a declaration of the will of God. He wants everyone to be saved, and this is not the only time scripture says so. In 2 Peter 3:9, it says:

The Lord is not slow to fulfill His promise as some count slowness, but is patient toward you, not wishing that any should perish, but that all should reach repentance.

Ezekiel 18:23 says:

Have I any pleasure in the death of the wicked, declares the Lord God, and not rather that he should turn from his way and live?

Many of us have quoted these passages with great joy. They encourage the proclamation of the Gospel to all, even to those who have sinned in the most grievous ways. Our God looks upon the sinful children of Adam objectively, taking note of our rebellion. He responds in longing love, wanting none to be lost in the great judgment to come. God loves all, and desires all to come to Him. It fills those of us burdened by our sin with joy and it spurs on the prayers we offer up for loved ones who are still in rebellion.

However, the clear statement in Psalm 115:3, that God does everything He wills, might leave us scratching our heads. If God is not willing that any should perish, and yet a great many are perishing, what is to account for this seemingly impossible-to-reconcile contradiction?

We have already discussed how often the "free will" answer is used to arrive at easy, unexamined conclusions. It is true that God gave human beings free will. It is also true that everyone who rejects the merciful offer of God's grace does so freely. So, does God have two different desires in this regard? Does He both desire them to be saved and desire them to have a free will? If so, it is not unlike the man who both wants to be famous and humble—eventually one desire will win over the other. Has God's desire that we have free will won out over his desire that all should be saved? And then, is God really like the one that Mick Jagger sang about? God doesn't always get what He wants?

Many Christians argue that God's desire that we have free will is greater than His desire that none should perish. They claim that He values free will over salvation and mercy. Is it true? Do the two wills of

God clash, with free will winning out over salvation? I do not think so. God Himself proclaims that He always gets what He wants.

Is God's will contradictory?

When we think there is no other answer than to pit God's desire for human salvation against His desire for human free will, we must consider the totality of scripture. We do well to quote more than our favourite verse. For if all we quote is that God is unwilling that any should perish, we may come to an incorrect conclusion about how God's will functions. When we consider scripture as a whole, we find many texts that fill out this matter of God's will. In the last chapter, as one among many examples of the complexity of God's concern for the lost, we considered 1 Samuel 2:25. The passage speaks about the rebellion and eventual death of Eli's sons: "But they would not listen to the voice of their father, for it was the will of the Lord to put them to death."

No mention is made of the free will of the sons of Eli. On the one hand, God wants all people to repent and be saved, including Eli's sons. On the other, He seems determined that they perish. Can we make sense out of these seemingly irreconcilable statements?

Let's resist superficial explanations. Good Bible students don't simply quote verses that agree with their position, they closely examine difficult passages. Consider that 1 Samuel 2:25 plainly tells us that God was unwilling to save the sons of Eli—and other passages say the same. Consider the often-read Romans 1:24: "Therefore, God gave them up in the lusts of their hearts to impurity, to the dishonouring of their bodies among themselves."

God willed men and women to be given over to their sins, leading to ever greater and more degrading sins.

Revelation 17:16–17 says:

> And the ten horns that you saw, they and the beast
> will hate the prostitute. They will make her desolate
> and naked and devour her flesh and burn her up with
> fire, for God has put it into their hearts to carry out his
> purpose by being of one mind and handing over their

royal power to the beast, until the words of God are fulfilled.

This means that when the antichrist and the false prophet bring carnage to the earth, it will be because it is the determined will of God that it should be so. This will lead to the eternal punishment of those involved, including the world leaders who've given themselves in service to the antichrist. God's will is that these earthly leaders be of one mind with the beast. God wills this.

If the reader is still unconvinced and thinks I am hunting for obscure Bible passages, let's multiply our examination of passages. Joshua 11:19–20 says:

> There was not a city that made peace with the people of Israel except the Hivites, the inhabitants of Gibeon. They took them all in battle. For it was the Lord's doing to harden their hearts that they should come against Israel in battle, in order that they should be devoted to destruction and should receive no mercy but be destroyed, just as the Lord commanded Moses.

It is apparent that the will of God as described in scripture is complicated—more complicated than an easy answer can address. That there are *two* wills in God should now be plain. On the one hand, God wills that *all* souls should be saved, on the other He turns His face against some, showing Himself unwilling to save. For this reason, to speak of the will of God without taking these scriptures into account leads to false conclusions.

God's will of decree and God's will of command

To speak of God's will in two different ways is not a new concept; many theologians of the past thought it necessary to make a distinction between a *decree* and a *command* of God, asserting that God may, for His own purposes, decree one thing while He commands the opposite. That is to say, God's will of decree is a very different matter than His will of command. Although we call both the will of God, the way in which a decree functions is very different than the way a command functions. A will of decree is that which is always done. A will of command is often not done. Hence, we can now confidently assert that Psalm 115:3 is a will of decree: "Our God is in the Heavens; he does all that he pleases."

When the Bible says that God does not will that any should perish, it is not using the language of His will of decree; rather, it is the equivalent of a command. God is commanding men and women to turn from their sins to be saved. The command says that, through the death and resurrection of Jesus, God has opened a way for whoever will to come. God asks, "Why would you die?" God wills, or he commands, that you come to him and be saved. But God has not *decreed* that it should be so. He may have commanded you to repent and believe, but we do not know if He has decreed it.

When God utters his will of decree, it is done without exception. In Heaven, God's will is *always* his will of decree. On earth, God's will is often his will of command.

What is the difference? In Genesis chapter 1:3, we hear God uttering His first will of decree: "Let there be light." God decrees that it should be so. It's not that God is saying that it would be a very good thing if there was light; rather, that light should come and it did. When God utters a decree, it is done. It is always carried out. It is never thwarted. Our God in the heavens does whatever He wants. There is light because He willed light. There is a universe because it was His determined will that a universe, and a planet named earth, and an environment with all its wonders and complexity should come into being. Whatever God decrees comes into being.

Let's contrast the will of God in creation with the will of God in the Ten Commandments. Exodus 20 begins with the words: "And God spoke all these words," and the Ten Commandments follow. First, He says: "You shall have no other gods before me." And what happened? Israel pursued the gods of the nations around them. The second commandment: "You shall not make yourself a carved image." And what happened? Idols were abundant in Israel. Eight other commands followed, including the prohibition against misusing His sacred name, the insistence that the Sabbath be honoured, the demand to honour one's father and mother, prohibition against murder and so forth. Not one command was kept. Indeed, the unredeemed human heart finds the commands to be burdensome. Even in the command prohibiting adultery, Jesus's Sermon on the Mount made it clear that we are guilty of adultery in the heart, whether we commit the physical act or not.

God's commands, His will for Israel and the world, have not come to pass. Why? Because God did not *decree* the ten commandments. He *commanded* them.

And so, when we read that God is not willing for any to perish, we need to ascertain what we are reading. We are not reading God's will of decree, for had He decreed that, it would certainly have been done. Rather, we are reading His will of command. God never decreed the salvation of all.

Why does God command things He does not decree?

Having established that God commands things that He does not decree, we next can examine whether God can command one thing and decree the opposite. Is this even possible? Indeed it is, and it occurs more frequently than we might imagine.

Let's examine Exodus 8:1:

> Then the Lord said to Moses, "Go in to Pharaoh and say to him, 'Thus says the Lord, "Let my people go, that they may serve me."'"

This is the will of command. The Lord is saying, "You, Pharaoh, are commanded to let my people go. This is what I desire that you do." But consider the previous passage, Exodus 4:21:

> And the Lord said to Moses, "When you go back to Egypt, see that you do before Pharaoh all the miracles that I have put in your power. But I will harden his heart, so that he will not let the people go."

This is the clearest example of a will of decree being in direct conflict with a will of command. Pharaoh is commanded to take an action, but God decrees that his heart is hard so that when Pharaoh receives God's will of command, he will resist that will. In this case we can clearly see that God commanded one thing but decreed the opposite.

Many find this to be stunning. I have been in Bible studies where people discussed this very topic. The usual question is, "How could God, who wants all men to be saved [will of command], at the same time decree that Pharaoh not let the people go? He knew the results would be tragic!" And they were. Egypt's economy eventually lay in ruins. Her most potent military force, her chariots, were wiped out in a single stroke. Not a home in the land was untouched by the death of the firstborn. Given that God decreed that Pharaoh's heart would be hard, clearly God, while He commanded Pharaoh to repent, decreed that these events would transpire.

So, given that God decreed Pharaoh's heart would be hard, was he acting un-righteously? To answer this, we need to study each incident in Exodus 4–14 regarding Pharaoh's hard heart. On six separate occasions mention is made of Pharaoh's hard heart without any indication of how it came to be that way. In chapter 7:13, we simply read: "Still Pharaoh's heart was hardened, and he would not listen to them."

On nine separate occasions we are told that it was God who willed Pharaoh's heart to be hard, meaning God so decreed it—which explains why Pharaoh would not listen. And as we have seen, whatever God decrees comes into being. However, just when we are tempted to think Pharaoh was hopelessly manipulated against his will, Exodus tells us that Pharaoh hardened his own heart—that is, he is the agent of his own unresponsiveness to God. For instance, Exodus 8:15 says: "But when Pharaoh saw there was a respite, he hardened his heart and he would not listen to them."

Pharaoh's will was that his own heart would be hard. He chose this freely. God's will was that Pharaoh's heart should be hard. God also chose this freely. The will of Pharaoh and the will of God were the same. How does this work? Consider the historical context. The Pharaoh of the Exodus, according to the Bible's dating system, was most likely Amenhotep II. We know from history that he was arrogant, handsome and successful in all he did. With that background, notice how God approaches him. On six separate occasions, while speaking with Pharaoh Moses refers to God as the "God of the Hebrews." In

Exodus 7:16, he says: "The LORD, the God of the Hebrews, sent me to you, saying, 'Let my people go.'"

To a man like Amenhotep, the most powerful man on earth, being commanded by a God of slaves was outrageous. It must have inflamed his already oversized arrogance. It made it seem that he, the most powerful man on earth, should be ordered to obey the God of slaves. If this God were powerful those men and women wouldn't have been slaves in the first place. The gods of the Egyptians certainly wouldn't fear a slave God. How much less would the man whose power the whole earth feared be frightened?

And yet, rather than calling him "the one true Creator" or "the God who truly exists" or even "the God of infinite power," Moses continues to insist on calling him "the God of the Hebrews." Moses referred to God in this way because God instructed him to refer to Him this way while in the presence of Pharaoh. And how that name for God must have made Pharaoh bristle and ask himself, *Do they really think I will submit to a God of slaves over the greatest civilization on earth?*

God was aware of how Pharaoh would hear these words. Indeed, God deliberately chose words that would further harden Pharaoh's heart, but having said that, we must not think God was manipulating Pharaoh's heart against his will. Instead, by speaking this way God was *exposing* Pharaoh's heart. God was showcasing the pride and arrogance of a man who lived for his own glory and aggrandizement. This is the method that God used to ensure this man who would not repent. God was determined to let him die in his own sin.

How many of us know what evil exists in our hearts? Given the right circumstances, we could all murder, enslave others and be wicked beyond all bounds. All that is required is for circumstances to uncover that which now lies dormant. But we have learned to hide these matters. Indeed, in his mercy God often protects us from circumstances that would allow great wickedness to pour from our hearts. But if God allowed for circumstances to reveal our greatest propensity to sin, we would surprise ourselves by what we are capable of doing!

In the case of Pharaoh, God decreed that he be exposed for who he was to both himself and his people. He hardened Pharoah, but not against his will. Pharaoh acted freely. But why? According to Romans

11, God did it to display to the entire watching world that he alone is God. By decimating Pharaoh and the Egyptians, God displayed to Israel, Egypt and all the inhabitants of Canaan that He alone reigns. Furthermore, this matter was recorded for all generations to read about and consider.

Because of Pharaoh's hard heart, many people came to understand that God alone is God, and that makes the hardening of Pharaoh's heart praiseworthy. God created the situation to safeguard his glory and to make the Gospel known to the greatest number of people. For my part, I am filled with praise and glad that Pharaoh's heart was hard, for had it been soft I might never have heard of the greatness of our God.

God rules over all things for the sake of His glory and for the good of those He has chosen as His own. When He commands one thing but decrees another, we have yet another reason to marvel at the wisdom of our God. When the Gospel of Jesus is under siege, when it seems like wicked men are on the rise and the Church is hard pressed, we must never lose hope. For as Psalm 115:3 insists, our God is in heaven and right now He is doing things exactly as He pleases. He may seem mysterious by commanding one thing and decreeing another, but these two wills are not contradictory; indeed, they are the means God has chosen to bring humanity to its final consummation. On that day God's will will be done on earth as it is in heaven.

Paul comments on the wisdom of God in Romans 11:33: "Oh, the depth of the riches and wisdom and knowledge of God! How unsearchable are His judgments and how inscrutable His ways!"

CHAPTER 8

Are We Fully Free?

Until now, I have said that human freedom, though real, is bounded by God. We are not free in an unlimited sense. Nonetheless, we do make free moral choices. But if God creates and sustains all things and is meticulously sovereign, how can human freedom be more than just an illusion?

Furthermore, as we have seen, God can harden and soften hearts at will. He hardened the heart of Pharaoh for His purposes and opened the heart of Lydia, whom Paul encountered in the Greek city of Philippi. Acts 16:14 says, "The Lord opened her heart to pay attention to what was said by Paul."

Additionally, Romans 9:18 says, "So, then he has mercy on whomever he wills, and he hardens whomever he wills."

Whatever can be left of human freedom? Do our choices matter? Are we truly free?

Do our choices matter?

I have been a pastor for many years. Because of my vocation I have tried to be conscious of the example that I set, particularly regarding moral issues, but in some non-moral issues as well.

I ride a motorcycle. I have ridden motorcycles since I was sixteen. I remember well the thrill of riding that first one and, amazingly, that thrill has never left me. But I am also aware that riding motorcycles on the streets and sharing the road with automobiles is dangerous.

One day, a woman in my church approached me to tell me that her sixteen-year-old son wanted to get a motorcycle. She and her husband had told him no. He responded, "Pastor John rides a motorcycle, so why can't I?" He was certain I would approve, and so his parents approached me for advice. I agreed to sit down with the young man and talk.

We met, talked and shared our love for motorcycles. I said, "It is very important to obey your mother and father, and while you are in their house you are under their authority." Then I had some questions. "What kind of bike do you want to get?" I asked him.

"I want a sports bike," he told me.

"They are dangerous rockets," I told him. "They limit one's field of vision and are most often the bike involved in fatal crashes. Perhaps you should tone down your aspirations. Perhaps you should even spend several years in an automobile, learning how traffic functions. And then maybe you might like to enroll in a motorcycle safety course. You would learn everything from lane positioning and control, to how to remain visible to people in cars, and this preparation just might save your life. Furthermore, once you have your licence your training hasn't ended. You will want to take any course you can to either update your training, or to better your skills. Motorcycles can be enjoyable, but they must be approached with wisdom and skill."

He interjected, "But, Pastor John, you said God is always in control, and he controls the day of your birth and the day of your death. So if God has already determined the day of my death, I don't see why I should worry about getting a motorcycle and riding very fast. Whether I ride fast or slow, my time of death is already determined."

I was impressed, even though he was a bit cheeky. Clearly, he had been listening to my sermons! He reminded me of myself at that age. I liked him. Here's what I said in response, "Yes indeed, God does determine the lifespan of each human being. But have you noticed that He always ends the lives of the dumb guys first? So smarten up!"

I could have added that our decisions and God's sovereignty are not mutually exclusive. If we put ourselves in needless danger, we may die. If we study hard in school, we position ourselves for a better future. If we drop out, we harm ourselves. All our decisions are meaningful. While the young man had grasped that God is the Creator and sustainer of all, and that He is meticulously sovereign over all things, he still needed to grasp that his choices were not meaningless.

It is immensely satisfying to note that God controls everything, from the birth of nations to the birth of mountain goats, from political governance to the way each living thing behaves. But none of that detracts from righteous or evil choices. Furthermore, God determines the course of each individual life, but that does not mean our decisions are irrelevant. Our choices both determine the course of our lives and make us accountable before God. Our choices are not irrelevant.

God determines the course of each life

God controls the footsteps of each person. We may decide the path we wish to travel, as well as the outcome we assume will result from our chosen path, but God determines every place we set our feet. Often, we may end up on a different path than we had planned. Many older people will tell that their lives turned out very differently from what they'd planned when they were young.

Some may be troubled by this, but there is no reason to be. If God's Providence is a kind one, the surprising twists and turns in our lives are part of God's loving design, and why would we reject the unexpected that God has designed for our eternal good?

God's meticulous control is a marvelous truth, and the weight of biblical evidence for it is surprising. Once our eyes open to scriptural teaching in this regard, we may be delighted. God is more involved in all things than we ever noticed. God no longer seems distant. We will begin to see His hand in each experience and encounter. There is never a time when we are not interacting with God. We may be unaware that we are doing so, but when we accept that He is directing the course of all things, our lives are revolutionized. We realize there are no chance encounters. We realize that both joy and crushing pain are directed by God.

While this truth causes joy to a great many, it causes deep uncertainty in others. Those who are not reassured continually wonder about the meaning of human actions. They ask, "If that is so, does it really matter if we choose good over evil? After all, God is running this show, so how can my decisions be even remotely meaningful?"

Some see this outlook as fatalism, and they drift into false teaching in reaction to the doctrine of Providence. One example of that is the false teaching of Open Theism. Open Theists argue that God doesn't know the future and it is not determined. From that perspective, they argue that God didn't know that Adam would have sinned. God may have thought it was a likely possibility, but He could not have known it with certainty. And so God could not have known that it would have been necessary to send His Son into the world. God also can't know how you will respond to the saving news in Jesus. Open Theists argue that God is far more knowing than we can imagine, and hence his anticipation of future events is better than ours. Still, He does not *know* the future. To them, the future is open. And it is this view, they believe, that prevents us from falling into fatalism or a determined future, where our choices don't matter.

The fundamental problem with this view is that the Bible says exactly the opposite. In 1 Peter 1:20, Peter is speaking about the redemption of believers: "We were purchased from the futile ways we inherited from our ancestors with the precious blood of Christ."

Then, speaking about Christ providing redemption on His cross, he adds: "He was foreknown before the foundation of the world but was made manifest in the last times for the sake of you."

Christ's redeeming work, which included His suffering for the sins of the redeemed, was already settled in the mind of God before anything was created. Notice how differently Peter and modern-day Open Theists think!

If we follow the logical outcome of Peter's statement, we would say that God both foreknew and *ordained* Adam's sin. Why else would He have created a world in which Christ's suffering had already been foreordained?

In Revelation 13:8, in a passage about the coming of the antichrist, we are given a clear indication that God knows exactly what is going to happen. In verse 8 we are told: "And all who dwell on earth will worship it, everyone whose name has not been written before the foundation of the world in the book of life of the Lamb who was slain."

This not only demonstrates God's perfect knowledge of the future, but his *ordination* of the future. Before the foundation of the world, God had already written His book containing the names of those who refuse to worship the beast in the future. These ones received eternal life, even before they were born.

The prophet Isaiah had the same view as that of Peter and John. In Isaiah 41:22–23, he mocks the idols many worshipped in his day, saying:

> Let them bring them and tell us what is to happen. Tell us the former things, what they are, that we may consider them, that we may know their outcome; or declare to us the things to come. Tell us what is to come hereafter, that we may know that you are gods; do good, or do harm, that we may be dismayed and terrified.

What Isaiah is saying is that what idols are unable to do, God does with ease. God tells us with certainty what is to come.

The biblical perspective is that God not only knows the future, but He knows it because he plans and determines it, sustaining and directing all things moment by moment. However, many Christians struggle to accept this, for if God knows and plans all things then does that mean we should abandon the concept of free will entirely? Are we then left with a faith that leads to a rigid determinism? Those who take this approach don't often seek to persuade others to know Christ, because they reason that if God wishes to save the lost He will do so without their involvement. This type of Christian often has little compassion for the suffering or needy, because they reason that God determines the future of every person, including those who live in misery.

Jesus told the parable of the Good Samaritan so we might be moved with compassion to act on behalf of the suffering. The Good Samaritan, upon encountering a man bleeding in the road, stopped and took him to a place where his wounds could be healed, and even paid his bills. Rigid believers, like the one I described above, think God's will is done if they step aside and let Him him work. They are not moved by compassion.

The doctrine of God's Providence is not reason for apathy; in fact, apathy is unbiblical. The call to expend great effort and sacrifice so that the Gospel might be heard and believed is a biblical call. There can be no apathy regarding the Great Commission. As Christians, it is part of our faith to reach as many people as possible with the glad and saving news of Jesus. Romans 10:14–15 says:

> How then will they call on Him in whom they have not believed? And how are they to believe in Him of whom they have never heard? And how are they to hear without someone preaching? And how are they to preach unless they are sent? As it is written, "How beautiful are the feet of those who preach the good news!"

Paul is clear: if we do not go, people will die in their sins. Jesus made it clear that the Gospel would be preached to all nations, and then the end would come. In that vein, 2 Peter 3:12 speaks of hastening the coming of our Lord. Peter means to say that, as we sacrificially give ourselves to the work of global missions, we are bringing the second coming closer. Imagine that! On one hand, the day of the Lord is determined by God, and yet by our efforts we hasten it! Which brings us back to free will. Clearly, the exercise of our free will is not an illusion.

The intersection of free will and divine sovereignty

Human beings really do have free will, and the decisions we make have consequences. The Bible teaches this, and Isaiah 55:6–7 makes it abundantly plain:

> Seek the LORD while he may be found; call upon him while He is near; let the wicked forsake his way, and the unrighteous man his thoughts; let him return to the LORD, that he may have compassion on him, and to our God, for he will abundantly pardon.

We would have to charge God with deceit if we were to argue that the free decision to forsake wicked ways and turn to the Lord for compassion was not real. We must choose! Either we choose to carry on in ways that pay no heed to the Lord, or we choose to humble ourselves and beseech Him for pardon. We must choose the ways of life or the ways of death. To those who prefer death to life, the prophet Ezekiel adds an additional plea in Ezekiel 18:31: "Cast away from you all the transgressions that you have committed and make yourselves a new heart and a new spirit! Why will you die, O house of Israel?"

Clearly, the Bible teaches both human freedom and God's Providence. Our task is to discover how these things can both be true. Where do these truths intersect?

How is God sovereign while humans choose?

To make sense of both truths, we use some philosophical concepts. Both God's meticulous sovereignty and human freedom are true and must not be denied. Is it possible to hold to both in a consistent and reasonable fashion? Can we joyfully embrace both without fear of contradiction? I think we can.

First, we must define what we mean when we speak of "free choice." We have already made the case that free choice is not unbounded. But we need to say more. How do we exercise free choice? What is the context of our choices? Is free choice the product of our loves and desires, the things we call affections? Or is it independent of those things?

Jonathan Edwards and Freedom of the Will

Jonathan Edwards' essay, *The Freedom of the Will*,[12] profoundly changed my thinking on this topic. The late theologian R. C. Sproul called this essay the most important theological work ever produced in America. I was a student in seminary when I first encountered it. It was assigned by one of my professors, Dr. Daniel Fuller. Each of us was to read it and demonstrate knowledge of the concepts it presented. At first I found myself lost in the language. But once I grasped both definitions of the terms Edwards used as well as the arguments he made, I found that my thinking had been transformed.

Edwards argues that freedom is the power of anyone to do as he or she pleases, and that, he suggests, is exactly what God has given us. But a complex series of thoughts arises from this. Edwards asks us to consider the *cause* of the things that please us, which he calls our

---

[12] Edwards, Jonathan. "The Freedom of the Will." 1754.

affections. For Edwards, the affections are the strong inclinations of our hearts. The heart determines what it is we love and hate, as well as those things to which we are indifferent. Whatever we love most motivates us to exercise freedom of will in that direction. But then Edwards makes a startling observation. He says we are only free to do that which our affections dictate. Or to put it negatively, we are bound from exercising any freedom in doing the things we despise. Under no circumstances can any of us do that which we do not desire. But Edwards goes even further. He adds that we are only free to do that which pleases us, and that we are prevented from doing the things which we despise. According to Edwards, under no circumstances can any of us do that which we do not desire. He also says we are not free to do what we view as a secondary motivation, at least not if we have opportunity to do that which we view as primary motivation.

Here is an illustration. Imagine it is a hot sunny day. There is an ice cream shop nearby with seventy-five available flavours. Can we freely choose any of them? On the one hand, says Edwards, we can; we are physically able to choose the one we prefer. On the other hand, the will is bound by its strongest inclinations (affections). If you passionately hate licorice ice cream, your inclination will direct you to avoid it. Furthermore, you will be directed by your strongest desires, meaning you must do what your soul loves the most.

This leads to an important question: is it true that we only do the things we please? Are we unable to do the things we hate?

Imagine a man who is a hopeless alcoholic. Let's personalize him by giving him a name: Jack. Jack's enslavement to alcohol has robbed him of everything. He has suffered a divorce, his children want nothing to do with him, he's lost his job and the bank foreclosed on his mortgage, leaving him homeless.

Imagine that Jack has just been gifted with a large bottle of very good scotch that a passerby has decided to give to him. The kind stranger carries on and Jack is left with the bottle. Is it a gift or a curse? Will Jack drink the bottle? Or, to put it another way, is Jack able to exercise his free will in such a way that he would be free to either drink the scotch or refuse to drink it? Just how free is Jack?

The answer depends entirely on what we mean by "free will." We might say, "Jack is perfectly free to refuse to drink the bottle." And we would be right in saying that. Jack is free to direct his body as it pleases him in what Edwards calls "physical freedom." No one is forcing Jack to drink. He is free to do as he wishes.

But consider Jack's freedom from a moral perspective. Jack may well be unable to refuse drinking that scotch because his will is captive to his "affections." In this situation, Jack finds that he must do what his soul loves more than other things. Alcohol supersedes all other loves in his life. This is his primary love, and it trumps wife, family, children, job and home. This is called "moral bondage." But in saying that, it would be unfair to say that Jack does not love his wife and children. We would be vilifying Jack to argue that he is unconcerned for them. He does love them. Furthermore, Jack would also love to get a job and be able to take care of himself and others. Jack would even love to be free from the enslavement of his addiction. But all of these loves are penultimate. His ultimate love is the sense of need he has for the alcohol.

Some might object to this description. Much work has been done to understand addiction. Addiction to alcohol changes body chemistry. It is no longer a matter of the will, but a matter greater than the will. But this is precisely my point. Every one of us is driven by matters greater than our will. The will is in bondage to do that which desires the most, whatever the source of that desire.

So to what extent is Jack a free moral agent? That depends on how one defines freedom. For Edwards, freedom is the power to do that which pleases us more than all other things. It is also the bondage of being unable to act *contrary* to that which pleases us above all other things. Edwards is saying that human beings, as free and responsible moral agents, always and without exception choose to do what they are most strongly inclined to do—meaning our volition is both free and determined at the same time.

Think about that: we are *determined* to do that which we are most inclined to do and we also freely choose what we want the most! This view of things has been called the "compatibilist" view of human freedom. Human freedom is compatible with God's meticulous sovereignty! We are free, but only in a certain sense. We are free to pursue our affections.

But we are in bondage to those very same affections. We are determined only to do that which our hearts love the most. Hence we are free, but we are also in bondage.

But God, knowing our bondage, is free to allow us to continue in bondage or to liberate us. Whenever He changes our heart in regard to sin, we are brought to value the cross and seek his face for forgiveness from our sin. This liberation is called "conversion."

Conversion to Christ and our freedom

I love to talk about my conversion to Christ in these terms. Before I knew Christ, I was acting in freedom. I freely hated God's laws and cast them behind me. I freely chose that which grieved the heart of God. And then, in wonderous mercy, I was presented with Christ's claims on my life. He was my Creator, hence my life was not my own. He was my judge, who had the right to judge every action I had ever taken. I learned His holy laws, and my heart was terrified because of my sin and because of his coming judgment. I learned of Christ's power to save me from my sin. I was given the freedom to confess my sins and lay my sins upon His cross. He died on the cross for my sins.

Before my conversion, I loved my sin. I know myself. Left to my own devices I would have chosen to reject the Gospel utterly. But God freely chose to cancel out my rebellion and give me a new heart. And now, blessed with a new nature replete with new affections, I freely choose to surrender my life and my lifestyle choices into the hands of Jesus my Saviour. In my conversion I see the confluence of God's freedom to choose, my bondage to my sinful affections, as well as the new heart with new affections that have been graciously given to me. Did I act freely when I came to Christ? Indeed I did! But had not God given me new affections, I would have refused him to this day.

The path we choose

Whatever path we choose in life, we do not choose it from some morally neutral position. We are not blank slates. None of us make decisions without reasons for making those decisions. We can without contradiction say we are determined to freely make the choices for the things our hearts love the most. Whenever we choose a path or make a choice or choose one thing over another, we do so for some reason. And the reason, says Edwards, rests entirely in what he calls the affections.

Romans 3:10–11 says: "None is righteous, no, not one; no one understands; no one seeks for God."

No one? Yes, no one. We rebel against God by nature. We do have a free will. Given the fallen and sinful nature of Adam, our free will is determined to reject God with all our hearts. In Adam we love making ourselves into gods rather than giving glory to God the Father. Sometimes we make decisions that shape our lives without understanding why. But the answer to that question is always a matter of the affections.

I wonder if you have ever said, "I don't know what possessed me to do that?" The answer to that question should now be obvious. You did that thing, because your affections overwhelmed your decision to do the opposite. Sometimes the choices we make are not of the moral variety, but they are always a matter of the affections. Perhaps you choose to take the scenic route home rather than the highway—you like this route because of the landscape. On a deeper level, maybe you're subconsciously delaying arrival home to avoid tension there. But however you made this choice, of this you can be certain: You did not choose to take this route home from a neutral heart, but from a heart that loves some things and rejects others.

Let's concentrate this discussion to the matter of our conversion. Ezekiel 36:25–27 says:

> I will sprinkle clean water on you, and you shall be clean from all your uncleannesses, and from all your idols I will cleanse you. And I will give you a new heart, and a new spirit I will put within you. And I will remove the heart of stone from your flesh and give you a heart of flesh. And I will put my Spirit within you and cause you to walk in my statutes and be careful to obey my rules.

When we convert to Christ, it is because God puts a new heart in us and causes us to walk in his "statues," meaning his way. Isn't that taking away our freedom? Not if you understand that freedom consists entirely in the affections. God doesn't take away our affections, he gives us affection for him that supersedes all other loves. That is true freedom. That is release from bondage, which can function so much like addiction. We let God lead instead of being slave to earthly pleasures.

However, true conversion and submission is not without many battles. All Christians battle between what the new spiritual heart wants and what the flesh (habitual patterns of rebellion) are used to. And so, as a part of Christian discipleship, we learn what Colossians 3:5 tells us to do: "Put to death therefore what is earthly in you: sexual immorality, impurity, passion, evil desire, and covetousness, which is idolatry."

Later, in verse 7, we are told that while we were non-Christians we walked in this kind of life. But why? Because our hearts were determined to. However, once we were redeemed our transformed hearts wanted something we had never wanted before: holiness. Instantly this new desire puts us into warfare with our earthly desires. The fight is a real one. Holiness comes only if we battle for it. We need to daily choose the way of Christ.

And so you see human choices are not an illusion, and neither are God's sovereign choices. Both are real and compatible with each other.

My choice is, "Thy will be done!"

I love to pray about the health of my heart. I love to pray Psalm 51:10: "Create in me a clean heart, O God, and renew a right spirit within me."

I love to pray, "Lord, change my heart daily so that I might love what you love. Unless you put love for you in my heart, I will despise you. I am dependent on you. If you do not choose to give me love for you, I will love other things. Dear God, choose to give me love for you, and I will choose to love you."

CHAPTER 9

Does Prayer Really Change Things?

Christians are both encouraged and commanded to pray. 1 Thessalonians 5:17 even commands us to pray without ceasing! To put it practically, we are to establish a regular routine of praying as well as uttering constant prayer to God throughout the day. This is to be the pattern by which we live our lives.

We are to pray because it brings us closer to God. Hebrews 10:22 invites us with the word: "Let us draw near to God."

The assurance that we will be accepted when we do so is a precious truth. Hebrews 4:16 says: "Let us then with confidence draw near to the throne of grace."

By his own blood, Christ has torn the veil asunder that hung over the holy of holies and boldly invited us to enter. We can say with confidence that God accepts the prayers of those who come in faith, and that prayer does change things. It changes *us* and makes us hungry for God.

But does prayer change the circumstances in our lives? James 4:2 says, "You do not have, because you do not ask."

This verse indicates that God will give us what we desire, if it is in keeping with his will, if we only ask. In Matthew 7:7, Jesus says, "Ask, and it will be given to you."

And in James 5:16, we read: "The prayer of a righteous person has great power as it is working."

John 14:13 promises: "Whatever you ask in my name, this I will do."

Many of us are familiar with these verses. They remind us that God is not a concept; instead, he is the living God who comes to the aid of His children.

In light of Providence, why pray?

Learning that all of God's designs are carefully crafted, and that no plan of God can be thwarted, Christians might well wonder what use it is to pray. As mentioned earlier, God determines the days of our lives before we are born, so what is the sense of praying for someone's healing? And yet, it may well be that God determines to heal someone through the prayers of His people. But it may also be that the illness will result in death. How are we to know whether our prayers will change the outcome?

Further complicating this matter are the instructions God gave the prophet Jeremiah. Jeremiah is known as the weeping prophet, for he lived in a day in which God was going to punish his people for their sins. He wept over this and also pleaded with the people of Judah to turn and repent. But no repentance was forthcoming. Disaster was coming. We would expect that before the disaster came Jeremiah would be in prayer, crying out to God that Judah might yet have a change of heart. And yet, three times he was told not to pray. Jeremiah 7:16 says, "As for you, do not pray for this people, or lift up a cry or prayer for them, and do not intercede with me, for I will not hear you."

In Jeremiah 11:14, he is told again not to pray: "Therefore, do not pray for this people, or lift up a cry or prayer on their behalf, for I will not listen when they call to me in the time of their trouble."

And finally, in Jeremiah 14:11–12, "The LORD said to me: 'Do not pray for the welfare of this people. Though they fast, I will not hear their cry, and though they offer burnt offering and grain offering, I will not accept them. But I will consume them by the sword, by famine, and by pestilence.'"

In Jeremiah we learn of a people who had been warned by many prophets in the past. Still, in spite of numerous warnings the hearts of the people were increasingly unresponsive to the God who called out to them. Now, in the time of Jeremiah the prophet is told that the opportunity to repent had passed. They had crossed a line.

When we read Jeremiah, we should reflect on Paul's words in Romans 2:4–5:

> Or do you presume on the riches of his kindness and forbearance and patience, not knowing that God's kindness is meant to lead you to repentance? But because of your hard and impenitent heart you are *storing up wrath* for yourself on the day of wrath when God's righteous judgment will be revealed.

The image of storing up wrath is terrifying. It assumes that God is recording each transgression against His law and keeping count. Some may carry on in sin and not face immediate judgment, but that is only because God has prolonged the opportunity to repent. This is mercy. It can also be a curse. Someone might misunderstand their experiences. God sends warnings, and in the present moment nothing changes. It is possible to interpret the lack of action on God's part as tolerance of sin. Hence, a cavalier attitude develops. God warns but does nothing. And yet, even while the warnings of God are mercy, the refusal to listen only stores up ever greater wrath. When the day of judgment comes it is exacerbated by the length of time between the warning and the judgment.

What if God's loving patience for someone is exhausted? Do our prayers extend the season of mercy offered for that individual? Or are we to not intercede as God asked of Jeremiah? And if Providence means God's will of decree cannot be altered, then what is the place of prayer? How are we to know if our prayers really change things?

Providence and prayer for others

Proverbs 20:24 explains that our steps are from the Lord and that we don't even understand our own way. Previously we learned that God lifts up one and puts another down. We learned that while God does not violate our freedom of will, He both hardens hearts and softens them.

God providentially oversees the ways of all men and women. Here we come to the point of our temptation. Why then should we then pray for anything? Does God not design each human life from beginning to end? How then shall we pray for mercy? Are not God's designs eternal? Can we think we will alter the eternal plans of the eternal one?

I hold that the Providence, when rightly understood, should cause God's people to pray *more*, not less. I can demonstrate with an example from my own life.

Some time ago, while on a trip guiding a group of pilgrims in the Holy Land, I received an alarming email. My son wanted my wife and me to know he had been diagnosed with cancer! Traumatized, I found a place where I could be alone. I wept. I pleaded with God to have mercy on my son. I then went to the public washroom, washed my face and dried it with a paper towel because I was scheduled to speak to the group a short while later and I was determined not to let anyone know of my son's plight, for the pilgrims on the trip had sacrificially spent a great deal to be on this trip. I worried they might become consumed with care for me and not with the joys of walking through the Holy Land. I kept the matter hidden between myself, my wife and my God.

When we returned home we immediately sought out our son, who told us he would not have discovered the cancer if he hadn't gone to the doctor to be tested for something else. He had been struggling with an unrelated health issue. The doctors discovered the cancer early—a blessing. He was operated on immediately and the cancer was removed. To this day it has not returned.

As I look back on that time my heart is overwhelmed with gratitude. God decreed that my son be medically tested for something else in order that this cancer would be discovered early and cured. Was that a miracle? No one laid hands on him, anointed him with oil or prayed, but by the time my wife and I returned from our trip he was already on the road to recovery. This was the hand of God directing matters for His glory, and His mercy for my son. It wasn't "lucky" that he went to see his doctor, it was the directing hand of God.

The skeptic may ask, "Why did God providentially direct matters so that there would be cancer at all?" But that is a failure to understand Providence. God *providentially directed* all these matters. Why? My best understanding is that He did this to allow me, my wife, my son, his wife and our extended family to know his grace. We needed a reminder exactly in line with the one we received.

As I write these lines, I am aware that other men and women's sons and daughters have died. Still others have suffered protracted illnesses. This has happened among families that have prayed as earnestly as my wife and I prayed for our son. They, like we, prayed in faith, urged to draw near the throne of grace through the blood of Christ. Some received a miracle. Some did not. What are we to make of this? Of this I am certain: God designs each detail for His glory and for the eternal well-being of his servants. This is so in joys and in sorrows. God is not absent from the lives of those who call upon Him.

This is equally true in less dramatic situations. We arise in the morning and find that we are still alive and in our right minds because God willed it. Therefore, we *must* worship. Prayer should not just be offered in desperate situations; part of prayer is to overflow with thankfulness and remain in adoration of God. Once we attune to it, we will no longer only occasionally see the hand of God, we will see it in every situation in our lives.

I once served a church that had a phone ministry. We called everyone twice a year, and thousands needed to be called. One of our phone volunteers was a man who was very much in tune with God's Providence at each moment. One day he called a wrong number. He apologized to the man on the other end of the line and said he was a part of a church phone team looking to pray for people in the congregation. After explaining that God directs all things, including his misdial, he asked if he could pray for this man about something. The man opened up instantly and revealed he'd been going through a difficult time. The phone volunteer prayed for him, and before long that man came to faith in Christ.

Was that a miracle? No, it was a moment of inattention and a slip of the fingers leading to a wrong number, but it was directed by the sovereign hand of God, who wills all things at each moment and transforms our lives and experiences. He even directs us when to pray, and with whom.

The Providence of God transforms every second and every encounter. To live this way takes us into a new arena. God is always at work. As Paul told the Athenian philosophers, "In Him we live and move and have our being" (Acts 17:28).

Prayer is a response to God

Prayer rises out of a response to living in our Father's world. It rises out a response of knowing, not just that God is involved in all things, but that his Providence is kind, and for all who believe. Prayer rises out of the reality that God has not treated us as our sins deserve. Rather, we are at all times the objects of His mercy. For this reason the prayers of those who believe are laced with adoration, thanksgiving and recognition that we are in the safety of God's loving hands. They are also earthly requests to a loving God who is aware of our weaknesses and needs.

But what shall we say when the outcome of our praying is such that we still encounter deep loss and pain, when the outcome is not as positive as it was for my son? If we believe God is meticulously sovereign, we may be tempted to blame and even curse Him. Job's wife felt that way after Job's wealth and physical assets were stolen from him. To compound his suffering, a great wind came and struck the house where Job's children were eating. All of them died in that incident. In Job 2:9 Job's wife says, "Do you still hold fast your integrity? Curse God and die."

Job's trials were not yet over. Job's health failed him and he became covered in loathsome sores. So grievous was his illness that when his own friends approached, they didn't recognize him. Here was a man who had lost everything—health, wealth and family—yet Job did not curse God as his wife suggested. In Job 1:22, it says, "In all this Job did not sin or charge God with wrong."

Two different responses, both coming out of great pain as well as an understanding that God was at the centre of the tragedy. To add to the opinions, Job's friends also weighed in, concluding that Job's misfortunes were because of his sin.

As the Book of Job unfolds, Job begins to question God. He wishes he could state his case and question God's actions. But as we approach the end of the book, God appears and, instead of allowing Job to question

Him, begins to question Job. "Where were you," he asks, "when I created the earth's foundation?" One question is added to the next. Job is unable to answer.

The point of God's questioning of Job is that He has complete knowledge and an eternal perspective. Our knowledge is fragmentary and often subject to error and contradiction. We must learn to pray with genuine requests, but we must also learn to pray with the head bowed in submission to the eternal love and wisdom of God.

Think again about Joseph, who was sold into slavery by his brothers. He believed that what his brothers had intended for evil had been intended by God for good. How can we cultivate that attitude? Knowing of God's Providence we can pray what Job prayed in Job 1:21: "The LORD gave, and the LORD has taken away, blessed be the name of the Lord."

Praying with faith on difficult days

God has ordained that his people should pray, even though He knows every aspect of every one of his children's lives. According to Matthew 6:8, Jesus said, "Your Heavenly Father knows what you need before you ask him."

We do not need to alert God to our needs, our fears, the dangers we face, the health crisis we endure or the financial needs we must survive. God already knows. He has no need for his children to remind Him. Furthermore, our prayers don't arouse his compassion. God is already gracious and compassionate and does not become more so. His compassion extends to us, to our families as well as to those we love. He already loves them far more than we do. Furthermore, we never need fear being honest with God when we pray for things that we know he intends to give us, such as forgiveness for sins. So confess and be humble and wait for Him to work in your life.

For a while, a false teaching was making the rounds that said, "We don't have to ask God for forgiveness, because Christ has already forgiven my past, present and future sins." The answer to this question has a great deal to do with the nature of prayer. First of all, we pray daily that God would forgive our sins simply because Jesus instructed us to pray this way. That in itself should settle the matter. Prayer is submission to the revealed will of God. We pray as we are instructed to pray.

But we may still wonder, "Why should I pray for something that has already been secured for me in the cross?" The answer is that the purpose of prayer is to create a relationship of faith. Prayer teaches trust and dependence on God, and God wants us to explicitly trust Him in all things. This is why we enter His presence and humbly confess that we have sinned, both in things we have done and things we have left undone, in things we have thought and longings we have cherished in our hearts. When we do this we are reminded of our propensity to rebel against our redeemer, and of his great mercy to us.

1 John 1:9, says, "If we confess our sins, he is faithful and just to forgive us our sins and to cleanse us from all unrighteousness."

Sin is an affront to God. Daily prayer and confession reminds us that God is gracious and compassionate, and that great love and grace flows from the cross of the crucified one. Prayer is about praise and the doctrine of God's kind Providence. Continual prayer helps us find more reasons for praise than we thought possible.

Asking and receiving

If God rules over all things, and if He not only knows the future but ordains the future, what point could there possibly be in praying for things that are already fixed in the eternal plans of God? What about asking and receiving?

James 4:2 says, "You do not have, because you do not ask."

If I understand James rightly, he seems to be saying that a failure in prayer keeps us from receiving what God wants to give us, and that God withholds until we ask. James adds in James 4:3: "You ask and do not receive, because you ask wrongly, to spend it on your passions."

It turns out that we must bring theology with us into our prayer lives because God will not allow us to simply name and claim anything we want.

Some years ago I went for a walk with a young man who, when it came to prayer, had been raised in the "name it and claim it in faith" school of thought. The idea behind this theology is the idea that faith operates like a spiritual force that always produces the results we verbalize. Those within this theology are constantly told to claim health and riches.

We passed a house that I loved. It wasn't overly large, but it was backed up against a forest and beautifully built. I said to him, "I just love walking by that house. It is one of the nicest I have ever seen."

My friend replied, "Ask God for it, and he will give it to you."

"I am shocked that you think of prayer that way," I told him. "Isn't it possible to simply enjoy the beauty of the house without desiring to possess it? Praying in this way treats God like a candy bar machine. You think your faith is like the money put into the machine. You select what you want and it always comes out at the bottom. What about the people who live in that house? What if they don't wish to sell? Should I pray against them?"

He was shocked. He had never looked at the consequences of such prayers. I added, "Perhaps we should pray for a change of heart?"

God wants our hearts to be in tune with His, and prayer is part of His training us to be that way. Prayer teaches us to love what God loves. My "name it and claim it" friend was right that I loved that house. He was also right to assume I couldn't afford it. It was beyond my reach. He was also right that I would have been overjoyed if I would have been able to purchase it. But prayer teaches us not to love this world nor the things in it. It teaches us to set our affections on the eternal Kingdom.

But let's get back to the issue of asking and receiving. Consider God's command to Israel from the very well-known passage of 2 Chronicles 7:14:

> If my people who are called by my name humble themselves and pray and seek my face and turn from their wicked ways, then I will hear from heaven and will forgive their sin and heal their land.

Notice the separate elements of prayer. "Humbling ourselves" refers to confessing that God is supreme, we are not, and we need him and are dependent on him. "Pray and seek my face" is desire to be in his presence. "Turning from our wicked ways" is repentance. In response,

God gives a promise: He will be attentive to the prayers of his people. He will heal their land and restore that which has been lost.

Prayer is learning the ways, will and purposes of God. It is not about somehow subverting God's providential designs to get what *we* want. It is about finding joy in that which God has intended for us. Prayer involves faith and teaches us to trust God. It also teaches us that our ways are often deficient. God, in loving Providence, has designed prayer so we grow toward Him.

Does prayer make a difference?

I can almost hear someone asking, "But does prayer really change things, or does it just change *me*?" Again we answer: both. As we saw in James 4:2, "You do not have, because you do not ask." We are encouraged to ask for change, in ourselves and our families, our churches and our nations.

Some things will never occur until believers ask. The Lord calls us to ask boldly, to plead with him for the salvation of the lost, for healing, for unity in our local churches, for wisdom in the leaders of our nation, for advancement of the Church throughout the world and, of course, for the health and safety of our families. But we also need to ask God for hearts that truly love him and his word. We must earnestly pray the prayer of Augustine who wished God to change his heart to obey whatever God commanded.[13] Augustine knew that he could not obey God's commands unless God willed that he would. To put it another way, we need to confess our human weaknesses and plead, "Change my heart O God."

Don't be afraid to bring your personal needs to God. Ask him for your daily bread. Tell him of the things that distress you and ask for relief. Tell God both what you need and what you want. For in bringing everything to God he will supply you with everything you truly need. Prayer is not at odds with a healthy doctrine of God's providential rule. Rather, understanding God's providential rule allows us to pray well.

---

[13] Augustine. *Confessions*. Grand Rapids, MI: Christian Classics Ethereal Library, n.d.

CHAPTER 10

Christians Are Not Fatalists

Some time ago, a local paper in my region referred to the march issue of *Sociology of Religion,* which suggested that approximately one third of Americans believe in God in a counterproductive way.

Since the newspaper in question is frequently hostile to the Christian faith, I was sure the study would target Christian doctrine, and I was right. The article suggested that Christians believe in fate, in predestination. That got my attention. The article conveniently lumped predestination with fate and, without defining either term, went on to say that a third of Christian Americans agreed that there's no sense in planning a lot, because their fate is in God's hands. Then it defined a healthy spirituality as being autonomous self-directed individuals who occasionally need a divine supportive companion, but not a God who directs our lives.

Are we to assume these were the only two options? Either we are fatalists or self-directed individuals? Is submission to the will of God a counterproductive spirituality? Is it really true that one third of Christian Americans need to be helped to abandon submission to the will of God? And furthermore, is self-directed morality healthy? Surely the world is already filled with people who have adopted self-directed morality. Are they all spiritually healthy? I maintain they are not.

This sort of indictment seems to be standard fare in the press. Confident trust in the God who rules all things, has declared His holy law, calls men and women to repent of their sins and offers His only Son as both Saviour and Lord is said to be counter-productive. I am

110

sure Ephesians 1:11 would seem to these researchers to be unhealthy spirituality. It says, "In Him we have obtained an inheritance, having been predestined according to the purpose of Him who works all things according to the counsel of His will."

Predestination or fatalism?

The newspaper article equated "predestination" with "fate." This is also a mistake a great many Christians make. I have often been asked if I believe in predestination. My response is by now well rehearsed. "Is predestination in the Bible?" I ask.

For those who can't answer this question, I answer for them. The word is used five times. The Bible affirms that we were *predestined* to conform to His image. I believe the Bible speaks truth in all cases, so I assume this to be the case.

We are well served to remember that God determined His people should live in submission to His will. We as believers repeat the words of our Lord daily, gladly saying, "Not my will but yours be done." These words are the opposite of acting autonomously. God does all things for *His* glory, not as means for us to do all things for our own. To think otherwise is sinful. We do well to remember that Satan's grand deception to Eve was that she could be like God.

William Earnest Henley, in his famous poem "Invictus,"[14] captures this sentiment of independence well. Humans love the idea of "me against the world," and so the poem became famous. He wrote, "It matters not how strait the gate, how charged with punishments the scroll, I am the master of my fate, I am the captain of my soul." In response, I offer the words of Paul from 1 Corinthians 6:19–20: "You are not your own, for you were bought with a price."

Our lives do not belong to us. As Christians, our rights have been surrendered to our Lord. He owns us, and we have become His slaves. When He commands us, we bend the knee. We are not autonomous. We are the servants of Jesus. Our lives are purchased by Christ our master. Hence we are not victims of fate, tossed like flotsam and jetsam on the sea. God rules, directs and sustains all things. The years of our lives are

---

14   Henry, William Ernest. "Invictus." 1875.

ordered by his design and the future is determined by the one who sent His Son for our salvation.

James 4:13–16 tells us:

> Come now, you who say, "Today or tomorrow we will go into such and such a town and spend a year there and trade and make a profit"— yet you do not know what tomorrow will bring. What is your life? For you are a mist that appears for a little time and then vanishes. Instead, you ought to say, "If the Lord wills, we will live and do this or that." As it is, you boast in your arrogance. All such boasting is evil.

Notice the interplay of human plans with the plans of God. The person in question is planning business ventures. He is not reprimanded for doing that. Human beings engage in business. What He is rebuked for is what He has left unsaid. He should have reminded himself that all His plans are subject to divine permission. The statement "if the Lord wills" is not merely a convention of speech, it is a reminder that whether we succeed or fail, whether we prosper or suffer want, all occurs at the discretion of God. God wills one person to rise to prominence and the other one not. None among us can resist His will.

The definition of fate

What is fate? It is the idea that all the events in life are predestined or predetermined. But this predetermination occurs either by alignment of the stars or by some other impersonal but natural force. "Fatalism" is a stark view in that it implies that we are helpless in the face of our destiny and cannot change it. Fatalism is akin to seeing humans as bugs floating down a river. Will there be calm waters or rapid ones? Will I sink or swim? A belief in fate makes planning irrelevant, for the forces acting upon the beetle are larger than all its efforts. It is being swept along towards its destiny. Whether it struggles against it or resigns itself to the future, the outcome is the same.

Such a view of things leaves people feeling helpless. They never know whether fate will turn out to their advantage or disadvantage. It is said that the belief in fate can help relieve stress. Perhaps so. If things are completely out of our hands there can be no point in stressing about them! But the belief in fate also leaves us feeling defenseless. And as the newspaper article said, it makes planning irrelevant. What will be will be. What you do doesn't matter.

With God in the equation, biblical predestination and fate differ greatly. To illustrate the difference, let's examine an incident found in 2 Samuel 10. The chapter describes a battle between the combined forces of Ammon and Syria fighting against Israel, which was under the command of King David.

The incident that led to war started off innocently enough. David had a warm, rich relationship with the king of Ammon, and there was peace and a lucrative trading relationship between the two next-door-neighbour nations. In today's terms, this is like Jordan being immediately east of the nation of Israel—and having a friendly neighbour to the immediate east who was important for Israel's security.

But then the king of Ammon died and was replaced by his son, Hanun. David realized it was important to be on good terms with the new king as quickly as possible. As a good will overture, David sent some key officials from his court in Jerusalem to Rabbah, the capital of Ammon, to express sympathy for the death of Hanun's father and to arrange an opportunity for the two kings to meet.

Somehow things went horribly wrong, and what started as a mission of peace and goodwill ended in mistrust and hostility. The new king of Ammon believed David's men were spies who were scoping his defensive weaknesses in preparation of attack. The relationship between Israel and Ammon immediately deteriorated. The Ammonites decided to teach David a lesson, and so they held David's men down, shaved off half of their beards, cut off half of their hair, cut their clothes in half and drove them out of their city, half naked and utterly ashamed.

In no time the two nations, once friends, were on the brink of war. The Ammonites quickly realized that Israel was militarily stronger than they were and hired 33,000 mercenaries from Syria, the enemy of Israel, as preparation against an attack from David. Inevitably the armies met on the battlefield and, before the battle began, David's chief commander, Joab, realized the combined forces of Syria and Ammon had secretly arranged their forces so that half were facing Israel from the front, and the other half was flanking them at the rear.

Israel was surrounded. Joab, recognizing that his army was in peril, made an instant decision about how to position his troops to deal with the threat. The situation is described in 2 Samuel 10:9-10:

> When Joab saw that the battle was set against him both in front and in the rear, he chose some of the best men of Israel and arrayed them against the Syrians. The rest of his men he put in the charge of Abishai his brother, and he arrayed them against the Ammonites.

Basically Hanun had two armies, Ammonites and Syrians, each under their own chain of command—a brilliant tactical move—surrounding Israel.

But Joab was not out of options. He quickly put together a small fighting force of his most elite, effective troops and commanded them to strike the Syrians hard, reasoning that since the Syrians were mercenaries who were only here for the money, a quick loss might dispirit them. He hoped that if enough of them fell fast they would fear for their lives, break ranks and run; after all, they had nothing to die for in this foreign land. Meanwhile, he placed his capable brother Abishai in command of the larger force, knowing the fight against Ammon would likely be a drawn-out battle.

The Syrians, just as Joab predicted, broke ranks first and fled when they were attacked. The Ammonites, seeing the Syrians in full flight, lost courage and they too fled the field of battle. Joab's strategy was sound. Israel won the battle decisively.

But recounting Joab's victory is not my reason for bringing up this historical incident. It is the final words Joab gave to his commanders and troops that is relevant here. Before we read them, let's remember Joab's brilliant strategy. His keen interpretation of what he faced is a testament to his intellect, calm composure and tactical brilliance. His strategy really did turn the tide in this battle. His assessment of the willingness of the Syrians and the Ammonites to fight and take losses proved remarkably insightful. But here is the point: after having done the best he could, Joab is still convinced that victory could not be assured. And so we hear him commanding his troops. 2 Samuel 10:12 records his final words before the battle is engaged: "Be of good courage, and let us be courageous for our people, and for the cities of our God, and may the LORD do what seems good to him."

Let's not miss the significance of Joab's final words. First, like a good leader, Joab encourages his men not to be dismayed because of the two armies that surround Israel. He wants his men to enter the conflict with courage and fight the battle with ferocity. But what he says next is not an afterthought. Joab has reasons for his men to fight with courage. "The LORD will do what seems good to him." This indicates that Joab is both a military general as well as a theologian. He believes that God will determine the outcome of the battle. The moments on which a battle turns will not be decided by the size of the opposition but by the gracious hand of God.

Of course Joab had reasons for confidence. He was aware that God had made eternal promises to Abraham regarding the nation that would come from his loins. Joab knows that Israel is the unique people of God. He knows that through Moses God had promised to give the land to Israel. Those cities for which his men were fighting were not just the cities where their loved ones lived, but they were also the cities of God's unbreakable covenant with his people. Joab no doubt took courage from the covenant God had made with Israel. This incident shows the vast difference between a belief in fate and in the meticulous sovereignty of God over all things. Yes, they must fight with skill and discipline. But as the battle grows in intensity, God and not the Ammonites will determine its outcome.

Isn't it interesting that confidence in God's rule didn't lead to placid resignation? Neither David nor Joab said, "Well, I guess whatever is supposed to happen is going to happen." They acted and took their places on the battlefield. Confidence in God's Providence led to courage and to calm, to sound decisions in the heat of battle. Joab calmly planned when others might have panicked. This is not autonomous humanity making its own decisions, nor is it fate; rather, it is certainty that servants of God need not fear the battle. Fate versus faith in a sovereign ruler are very different things.

Providence and action

Belief in Providence leads us to action rather than passive acceptance. Men and women of faith never say, "There is no reason for plans or for action, because whatever is supposed to happen is going to happen." Instead, their confidence that God controls all things leads to courage. David thought so. Psalm 18:27–29 records David saying:

> For you save a humble people, but the haughty eyes you bring down. For it is you who light my lamp; the LORD my God lightens my darkness. For by you I can run against a troop, and by my God I can leap over a wall.

Strong confidence that God is both Creator and sustainer takes away thoughts of failure, for if our plans are undertaken for the glory of God and His eternal purposes, His wisdom and courage will guide us. Providence leads to acting, doing, working hard, being courageous and never giving up. This is as true now as it was during the days of the First Testament.

We find this same attitude present as the Gospel of Jesus is being preached in the world. In Acts 18, Paul's missionary activities in the Greek city of Corinth are recorded. At that time Corinth was the largest and most influential city in Greece, as well as an important city in the ancient Roman Empire. Paul had been planting churches in the Roman province of Asia, but God intervened and sent him a vision that changed his life. In the vision a Macedonian man stood before him, begging Paul to come to Macedonia in northern Greece, and so Paul crossed the Adriatic Sea and begin planting churches in Europe instead. This vision also changed the world; we can confidently say that it brought Christianity to Europe.

Paul, ever mindful that he was a slave of Christ Jesus, believed he had been set apart for the Gospel before he was born. He believed he was predestined for Christ! Without question he went with that attitude to Macedonia, landing first in the port city of Neapolis. From there he walked inland to Philippi, the largest city in Macedonia, and won his first European convert to Christ, a woman named Lydia. Many others followed. But his activities came to the attention of the authorities, and the growing Jesus movement was seen as a threat to Greco-Roman culture. Paul was arrested, beaten and thrown into prison. He was released only after he had preached the Gospel to the prison jailor and witnessed his salvation. However, city officials threw Paul out of town.

Still bearing the wounds of lashes, Paul went south on the Greek Peninsula, to the city of Thessalonica. There a jealous mob from the synagogue created an uproar at his presence, and so Paul's companions quietly snuck him out of the city one night.

He continued south and soon arrived in the smaller city of Berea, where the audience was more receptive. In Athens, which was next, he won only a few converts because the city was full of idols and the philosophers thought him ignorant. He was called a "babbler," but that did not deter him from his course. He set sail again and finally arrived in Corinth at the south end of Greece.

Arriving in Corinth must have been a bittersweet experience. By the time he got there his obedience to the vision God had sent him had cost him considerably. He had been imprisoned, scourged with Roman whips, mocked in public and discounted as a public nuisance. He had become a disturber of the peace and enemy of the state, yet he had soldiered on. Clearly Paul was not an autonomous man, nor one who simply believed that "whatever will be, will be."

One wonders what Paul's state of mind was when he finally arrived in Corinth. Corinth was the most important city. Corinth was the prize. If the Gospel took root in Corinth, it would influence all of Europe. In 2 Corinthians, he said that his state had become so precarious he despaired of life itself. Clearly the great apostle was fragile. At this moment, God intervenes. Acts 18:9–says:

> And the Lord said to Paul one night in a vision, "Do not
> be afraid, but go on speaking and do not be silent, for I
> am with you, and no one will attack you to harm you,
> for I have many in this city who are my people."

The Lord reassured him with a very curious phrase: "I have many in this city who are my people." What can that possibly mean? In the New Testament, those who are His people are those who have come to believe in the Gospel. But we know that the Gospel had never been heard in Corinth before. Paul had come to bring it. What must Paul have concluded from those words? It could mean only that God, who directs and controls all things, had *predetermined* that a great company of men and women would be saved in Corinth. God had planned great success for the Gospel in this city.

But knowing this doesn't make Paul passive, it wakes him up. He gets right to work. Very quickly opposition to his work is felt. But he is undeterred. God has promised him he will not fail in this city. He spreads the word at a synagogue and gets kicked out, but not until he has won some of the Jewish people to faith. He then sets up a base of operations in the house of a Roman man named Titius Justus. He finds a place to hold worship services. He begins actively preaching the Gospel. He trains up key leaders. Opposition toward him continues to grow, but he is undeterred because God has promised him that he will not fail.

All in all, Paul stayed in Corinth for a year and a half, working night and day to bring the Gospel to the people. When God told Paul that he had already arranged for the conversion of a great company of people, he did not sit on his laurels and think, *God has this, I don't really have to work so hard.* Instead, his attitude was that if God was arranging for a successful church, he should work *harder* to ensure it happened. How could he fail? If God was for him, no one could be against him. God's Providence provided him with the same courage Joab had when he spoke to his army to reassure them.

Paul had great faith in God controlling all things. This is recorded in his last letter, written shortly before his execution in Rome. Paul wrote to his young disciple, Timothy, to tell him he had been treated like a criminal for preaching the Gospel. But in 2 Timothy 2:10, he also says, "Therefore, I endure everything for the sake of the elect, that they also may obtain the salvation that is in Christ Jesus with eternal glory."

Does that strike you as a strange statement? He speaks of those he has come to share the Gospel with as the "elect" or "chosen." What this means is that God elected them before Paul even got there. Those who come to Christ have been elect. Paul believed that. In Ephesians 1, he tells believers they were chosen "before the foundation of the world."

And in Romans 9:16 he assures believers that their salvation doesn't depend on their own weak wills, but on the will of God.

Paul never wavered from this position, and yet rather than passively sitting back and saying, "I guess God's will is going to be done," he says, "Since God already chose the elect, I will endure everything for them. There will be no end to sacrifices and effort on my part. I will push forward until God, in His Providence, calls me home."

How Providence and human effort work

We do well to understand how the Providence of God and human effort work together. Paul offers a solution in Romans 10:14-15. We have seen before that Paul writes:

> How then will they call on Him in whom they have not believed? And how are they to believe in Him of whom they have never heard? And how are they to hear without someone preaching? And how are they to preach unless they are sent? As it is written, "How beautiful are the feet of those who preach the good news!"

Let's follow this progression through. God is determined to save a great company of men and women. However, they can't be saved unless they hear the Gospel, repent and believe. But they can't do that if they have never had anyone explain the Gospel to them, and so a preacher is key for their salvation. In his providential designs, God raises up preachers, teachers, evangelists, missionaries and faithful men and women who share the Gospel wherever they go.

Please observe that the way in which God executes his providential designs is through creating a people who are willing to obey their Lord and carry out his commands. Joab knew it on the battlefield, and Paul knew it as he entered Corinth. God's providential designs never make us passive, they make us active.

When I was a child there was a program on television called *The Doris Day Show*. It always began with Doris singing a song called "Que Sera, Sera," which loosely translates to, "whatever will be, will be." It was a cheerful song about fatalism, and its message was that what happens does so because it was meant to, though randomly and not necessarily at the hand of God. People who believe in God's Providence never talk that way. They talk about God's appointed designs. They speak of divine meetings with key individuals. They speak of possibilities that open because God has designated that they do so. They seize opportunities provided by open doors, believing it was God who opened them. And they see themselves as engaging in missions that won't fail because God has willed them. They bring courage to every battlefield.

When the great missionaries of the past went out, they did so because of a deep inner conviction that Christ had called them to go, and to be fruitful. The history of protestant missions shows us that these same men and women believed God would give them success, and so they sacrificed everything. That's the difference between belief in fate and confidence in God.

CHAPTER 11

For His Glory and Our Good

It is possible to react negatively to the news of God's meticulous sovereignty. Some of those reactions may be the result of deeply painful personal experiences. That God directs these events is hard for many to bear.

Years ago I was discussing the faith with a woman who was hearing the Gospel for the first time. It was an important conversation. In tears, she told me about her brother's descent into depression and darkness, which culminated in his suicide when he shot himself. The woman, who was considering becoming a Christian, wanted to know if God was watching as her brother took his life. "How could He do that," she asked, "and not intervene?"

Of course, I had no answer as to why God did not intervene or give her brother a change of heart, but I did affirm the validity of her question. I told her, "God had never taken his eyes from your brother, both in his joy and in his sorrow." She nodded. She told me she would need some time to absorb this. She had to find out whether the presence of God was to be welcomed or feared. Was the watching God a good God? Eventually this woman came to faith, believing that the watching God was indeed good.

Many people stumble over the idea of God's omnipotence (all powerful) and omnipresence (all knowing), especially when inexplicable things happen. Job struggled with this. God's steady gaze disturbed him. He called God, "You watcher of men." In Job 7:19 he asks, "How long will you not look away from me, nor leave me alone till I swallow my spit?"

At that time, in Job's misery he would have preferred that God allow him to suffer without his gaze upon him; indeed, Job wanted God to look away just long enough so he could swallow his own spit. Even that request was not to be. God's gaze was constant.

God's presence and benevolence

God is the Creator and sustainer of all, which is reason for great comfort. But it can also be reason for confusion, and even anger. As a pastor, I speak of these things all the time. Once, in a conversation with a woman dying from a debilitating disease, I was asked, "Did God will this?"

I hesitated to answer, but she was unwilling for me to deflect. Eventually I said, "Yes, God sustains and directs all that exists."

Her reply overwhelmed me. She said, "Good! If I did not know my loving heavenly Father was directing this, I don't believe I could endure it."

But I have heard the opposite as well. One man, who was distraught after the death of his son, told me that if God was part of it he would never make peace with Him.

Christians need to understand that the Providence of God is not indifferent or cruel. Despite specific events that might cause us to rage or suffer or grieve, everything rests on the truth that God's providence is good and loving. The Bible assures us that it is so in Romans 8:28: "And we know that for those who love God all things work together for good, for those who are called according to his purpose."

Several things are essential.

First, God makes no promise of His eternal good to those who are not called according to his eternal purpose. Does that mean that God is not good and loving to those who do not confess Christ as Lord? We will need to return to this question.

Second, the promise of Romans 8:28 is not a promise for our *immediate* good, meaning our temporal and worldly good. All things most definitely do not work together for our temporal or worldly good. God's promise is an eternal one. Were it not for the promise of the resurrection, we would be of all men most to be pitied. Hebrews 11 tells us of heroes of faith who have been tortured, mocked, flogged, imprisoned, stoned and sawn in two. It is impossible to apply Romans 8:28 to anything but our eternal long-term good, and so those who teach that faith is the key to riches, excellent health and so on are getting it wrong at best and deceiving us at worst!

God has the best possible eternity in mind for His servants. For that reason He watches over all we experience so that it all contributes to our long-term good. But what of unbelievers? Is God good to them in any sense?

God's kind Providence toward those who do not believe

I am a connoisseur of folk music, and I seek out songs that few others listen to, songs that have both good music and meaningful lyrics. I was recently listening to Canadian singer/songwriter Garnet Rogers, who wrote a beautiful ballad and love song called "Summer Lightning." It is the story of a man on a road trip whose senses are alive to the splendours of the natural world as he simultaneously thinks about his sweetheart at home. He marvels at both the wonders of the world around him and the wonders of the woman he loves. Then Rogers sings of the brevity of life, and how moments of beauty and joy are fleeting.

His lyric reflected the Scripture truth about the brevity of life. Job complained that his days passed by more swiftly than a weaver's shuttle. Moses said our days are like desert grasses: new in the morning but withered by nightfall. James asked, "What is your life? A mist that appears for a little while and then vanishes." The image of summer lightning is indeed an image that makes sense. How briefly we appear, and then walk here no more.

But the song's conclusion puzzled me. It stated that even though life passes like a flash in the night, love remains. I wondered, *But how can love remain?* If we pass away as swift as a swallow's flight, how can *anything* remain? Is it not true that without faith all we are and have done, all we loved and have hated will not only soon be gone, but will never be remembered? Rogers should have sung, "Nothing remains, not even the love we presently share." Ah, but that thought is too harsh for many.

But Garnet Rogers was not done. The song asks the most obvious of questions. Why is there a world? Why does that world stir the heart and emotions with its beauty? What is the explanation of this? And then, inexplicably, Rogers refused to answer his own question. His lyric ends with a shrug of ignorance and apathy. All the singer cares about is that the woman he's pining for loves him.

I was stunned by the flat ending of what was otherwise a beautiful song. I wanted to scream out, "Yes, you do know who created this world, but you don't want to confess it and so you banish it from your lyrics! In the end, the one who drew the curve in the magpies' wings and the one who shaped your life and the life of the woman you love will remain. But your love will perish along with all other things." A lovely song with well-written lyrics, but in the end, utter folly.

In Romans 1:19–20, Paul says:

> For what can be known about God is plain to them because God has shown it to them. For his invisible attributes, namely, his eternal power and divine nature, have been clearly perceived, ever since the creation of the world, in the things that have been made. So, they are without excuse.

Paul goes on to say that the willful suppression of that which is self-evident results in a lack of gratitude for his gracious provision. Darkness closes into our thinking and God gives us over to our worst impulses. Then the rest of Romans 1 talks about sins and vices, to which God hands over those who will not offer Him their gratitude.

But is this all God does to those who do not believe? Does God merely abandon sinners to sin? For if we observe the affairs of human beings around us, we will see much more than simply people abandoned to darkness. It may be true that singer Garnet Rogers refuses to acknowledge that the nature he enjoys comes from the hand of God. But God has clearly given him musical gifts and creativity. Is not this the gracious hand of God to those who do not believe?

Psalm 104:13–15 demonstrates God's faithfulness to the entire human race:

From your lofty abode you water the mountains; the
earth is satisfied with the fruit of your work. You cause
the grass to grow for the livestock and plants for man to
cultivate, that he may bring forth food from the earth
and wine to gladden the heart of man, oil to make his
face shine and bread to strengthen man's heart.

God provides all these things regardless of our response to Him.
It is His gracious goodness. Paul calls God the Saviour of all people
in 1 Timothy 4:10. He is not speaking of salvation from sin and his
gift of eternal life; rather, he is saying that God is good to all. God
repeatedly saves human beings from their worst impulses, from disaster,
from famine and from any number of dangers. The same sentiment is
expressed in Psalm 145:9: "The Lord is good to all, and his mercy is over
all that he has made."

Similarly, Matthew 5:45 records Jesus as saying, "For he makes his
sun rise on the evil and on the good and sends rain on the just and on
the unjust."

Imagine two farmers living beside each other. One rises in the
morning and his first thought is to thank God for the new day, the
health he enjoys and the fertility of the land he farms. The other farmer
awakens and curses God for a day of hard work ahead of him. And yet,
in his providential goodness, God sends rain and sunshine onto both
men's fields, and both reap a plentiful harvest.

God is good to all. This earth is blessed by goodness. The sun rises.
The seasons pass. The earth is filled with bounty. Men and women are
blessed with intellect, talent, strength and ingenuity. God's providential
care truly does fall on the just and the unjust. It may be a sin-cursed
earth, but it is also a beauteous and bountiful one. But God's care for
people does not carry on indefinitely. The night is coming, and with it
comes the judgment of God. God has ordained it so, in order that we
might consider our ways and look for a saviour.

The viewpoint of partial deism

We have previously mentioned a theological alternative to the doctrine of God's kind Providence in chapter one called *partial* deism. In this view the universe functions according to natural laws and God permits these laws to carry on, observing each detail. Partial deists agree that God meticulously, moment by moment, sustains the world and is Creator, but unlike deists (who deny God's intervention in all things), they admit He intervenes and adjusts the natural order of things in numerous ways, occasionally through miracles or intermittent acts of Providence.

For a great many, this idea is preferable to that of meticulous providential care. This view, they think, better explains perplexing things such as why some God-deniers live long and prosperous lives while some faithful followers of Jesus live lives of great trouble. Perhaps, they say, God allows human lives and civilizations to develop on their own, even while it does so under His watchful care. From this perspective, the reason unbelievers are often greatly advantaged in this life, is not that God has willed it to be so, but rather that the creator allows them to do so apart from his intervention.

Consider three examples from 2 Chronicles. In chapter 10, Rehoboam (son of Solomon) becomes king of all of Israel, including Israel to the north and Judah to the south. Rehoboam has inherited the nation from his father, King Solomon. It is as rich and as powerful as it has ever been. But Rehoboam makes the mistake of losing touch with the people, and that leads to catastrophe. In 2 Chronicles 10:15, it records, "So, the king did not listen to the people, for it was a turn of affairs brought about by God that the LORD might fulfill his word."

Rehoboam appointed a new set of advisors who were out of touch, and instead of listening to his frustrated people, he listened to the advisors. That mistake proved costly: it resulted in the partition of the nation, which would never be healed. The author of 2 Chronicles makes clear that the young king's costly mistake was brought about by God. God did not stand back and let the culture of Israel and the political decisions of unwise rulers take care of themselves. Rather, he purposely directed this matter.

Several chapters later, in 2 Chronicles 18:22, we find another example of God's direction: "Now therefore behold, the LORD has put a lying spirit into the mouth of your prophets."

And later again, in 2 Chronicles 25:20, we read, "But Amaziah would not listen, for it was of God, in order that he might give them into the hand of their enemies, because they had sought the gods of Edom."

Repeatedly we see God meticulously involved in mistakes, in inattention, in seeking false spiritual signs and in the false pride of kings. God is directing all these rebellious acts. Partial deists have misunderstood God's involvement.

We are left with this biblical conclusion: when unbelievers prosper and are blessed, it is because God has willed this for them. When unbelievers suffer, they do so because God has willed this for them. God wills all things.

God's eternal kindness to those who believe

Christians are called upon to give thanks to God *in all things*. I have occasionally heard Christians say that we are to give thanks *in* all things, but not *for* all things. This view is not biblical. Ephesians 5:20 admonishes us to "give thanks always and for everything."

In Paul's way of thinking there is not one thing he has experienced that has not been an occasion for which to give thanks. Whatever occurs has done so because a God who wants the best for him ordained that it should occur. Paul assumed that God had ordained all his experiences. It is true that he would not have always been aware of the long-term good that would be wrought through each experience. How could he know the eternal plans of God in all things? But he could rejoice that a good and benevolent God has an eternal purpose.

Reflecting on the wisdom of God in his dealings with his people in Romans 11:34–36, Paul says:

> For who has known the mind of the Lord, or who has been His counselor? Or who has given a gift to Him that He might be repaid? For from Him and through Him and to Him are all things. To Him be glory forever. Amen.

Notice the three affirmations. First, Paul affirms that all things are *from* God. God is the Creator, and nothing exists or can exist without it coming from him. Second, Paul says all things are *through* him, meaning all things are directed by God's infinite wisdom and with care. Ultimately, he says that all things are *to* him. All things that exist redound to God's glory.

God never has to explain away or apologize for any occurrences in His universe. He is not embarrassed by any event. Rather, each event that occurred in all history will be on display as an example of the perfections of His attributes. When the saints finally enter glory and are invited to examine all of history, they will be filled to overflowing with the wonder of all that has occurred. Not one event will be exempted. No event will cast aspersions on God's rule over all things. All events will glorify Him. This will include the examination of all big things and all small things. What once seemed of major importance and of no significance at all (the falling of a sparrow to the ground) will all be given as evidence for the undiminished splendour of God.

This must also refer to every experience each believer has. If God determines the long-term eternal joy of each child of God, we can imagine that He will invite the elect in heaven to examine and re-examine every one of their experiences. They will receive fresh understanding of how their experiences were designed by God to maximize the joy they are now experiencing. That reflection of their earthly lives will be the cause of great joy in heaven.

But what are we to make of our own sin? Can we say of our sins that even they redound to God's glory? But here we must exercise caution in our thinking. In 1 John 2:15–16, the Bible teaches:

> Do not love the world or the things in the world. If anyone loves the world, the love of the Father is not in him. For all that is in the world—the desires of the flesh and the desires of the eyes and pride of life—is not from the Father but is from the world.

This creates a conundrum, as in one sense everything is from the Lord, but in another sense it is not. How can both of those things be true? When Joseph told his brothers, "You intended it for evil but God intended it for good," he was indeed saying a mouthful.

Think of our sins in this way. God could have at any moment given us the wisdom and power to avoid every sin. That does not absolve us of any sin we have committed. After all, sin is our declaration of war on the holiness of God. No sin is *from* God. Furthermore, all sin in a believer is intended for evil. But God in His kind providence did not intervene to stop us. He had intent in this. He intended to allow sin to remain for a season for a greater purpose.

As we said in chapter six when we discussed evil, when we say that all things are from God, we are not saying that sin comes from Him. We are saying that sin remains because God has willed that it would do so at each moment. And that it is all a matter of intent. The sinner intends to do evil. God intends to do good.

Notice from Romans 11 that, since all things are from God, Paul hastens to add in verse 35 that no one can give to God so that He has to repay us. When we do good, it is possible because it was sustained by God. All things come from God. Therefore, rightly and justifiably, God takes credit for all good that occurs. There are no random acts of kindness. There are only acts of kindness that are sustained by God.

Paul then adds another point. Since all things come from God we know that He is in no one's debt. Therefore no one can give counsel to God. In Romans 11:34, Paul says, "For who has known the mind of the Lord, or who has been his counselor?"

Paul is asking, "What advice will you give God regarding the way in which he sustains all things?" This rhetorical question really means, "How can one pretend to know more than an all wise God?" When we wonder why God has allowed a specific event to happen, we are questioning the wisdom of God. God does not need our counsel.

Here is wisdom: don't counsel God! Don't give Him advice. Don't attempt to instruct Him in wisdom. Don't presume you can correct His ordering of all things. Don't even complain. Isn't it enough that He has promised you Romans 8:28?

God understands everything that is for our short- and long-term well-being. Let me provide an example. I set aside money every month, so that when I retire I can live off my savings and expect a decent quality of life. This is long-term planning for my long-term good. But that long-term good runs contrary to my short-term good. It is in my short-term interests to use that income today. And so I must decide which good I wish to pursue—short- or long-term?

"Short-term pain for long-term gain" is the credo of gym rats everywhere, and it is solid advice. Peter gives the same advice in 1 Peter 1:6–7, when he talks about our final reward in heaven:

> In this you rejoice, though now for a little while, if necessary, you have been grieved by various trials, so that the genuineness of your faith—more precious than gold that perishes though it is tested by fire—may be found to result in praise and glory and honour at the revelation of Jesus Christ.

For this reason, no one who puts his or her hope in Christ will want their best life now. We want our best life in *eternity*. Everyone who understands the cross knows that Jesus despised the idea of forsaking his shame and torment (short-term pain) on the cross, because he knew his true reward (long-term gain) was at his Father's side in heaven. Hebrews 12:2 says, "Who for the joy that was set before him [long-term joy] endured the cross [short-term suffering], despising the shame."

Since God knows what is in our long-term interest, it is important for us not to assume that we are his counselor. Since God prefers our best life in the world to come, let's not attempt to tell him how to arrange his providential designs. For this reason we do well never to indulge in the game of "what if" or "if only." Instead of a life of disappointment and regret, let's live with assurance that God uses all our experiences to work for our eternal good and for His glory.

When we reach the end of our lives, there will be no point in berating ourselves for not achieving things that we thought we could have. The believer trusts in God. A true believer will think, *The only thing I wish I could have done differently is to not have sinned. All other things, even the consequences of my sin, were of God's purpose. I am content.*

The last part of Romans 11:33 says, "How unsearchable are his judgments and how inscrutable his ways!"

If we constantly question God we bring trouble to our souls. Instead, we need to remind ourselves of Deuteronomy 29:29: "The secret things belong to the LORD our God, but the things that are revealed to us belong to us and to our children forever."

In his infinite wisdom God chooses not to reveal all his purposes, but he reveals some things. He has revealed that all things do work together for the good of those who love Him, in all circumstances.

God has never forsaken his people.

CHAPTER 12

Providence Says, "Fear Not"

1 Samuel 15 records one of those pivotal moments in the history of the Kingdom of Israel. Saul, son of Kish, from the tribe of Benjamin, was anointed Israel's first king. One of his tasks was to defeat the Amalekites who threatened Israel. Saul accomplished that, demonstrating that he was an able king and commander of the military.

But in victory Saul did not obey God's command that all the spoils of war be utterly destroyed. Israel was not to gain any benefit from this victory, it was all to be devoted to the Lord, to utter destruction. Saul decided against the Lord's will. He chose to destroy only worthless things and to keep valuable ones. He gave the best of the cattle to his men as payment for their efforts in battle and he spared Agag, the king of the Amalekites, as well as the best of the livestock.

Saul made this decision because livestock was valuable in ancient times. Agriculturally based societies needed livestock, and livestock equated to wealth. But his decision showed a lack of faith in God's provision as well as an unwillingness to obey.

Eventually the prophet Samuel showed up and roundly denounced the king's blatant act of rebellion against God. Samuel announced that God was so angered by King Saul's disobedience that He was going to remove Saul from the throne. This was a pivotal moment in both Saul's life and in the history of Israel. Hardly had Saul become king when it was announced that he would be a transitional ruler. Saul and his family line would be rejected. Eventually David would become Israel's great king.

To understand Saul's disobedience it is critical to understand his motivation. When confronted by Samuel about such blatant disobedience to God, Saul offers up his reasons. In 1 Samuel 15:24 we are told, "Saul said to Samuel, 'I have sinned, for I have transgressed the commandment of the LORD and your words, because I feared the people and obeyed their voice.'"

Saul was afraid that if he obeyed God and denied his people the booty of war, anger against him would be the result. At the time of his coronation there were already men who doubted his leadership. His men felt in this instance that, because they had risked their lives in battle, the spoils of their enemies was their rightful due. Saul reasoned that his obedience to God might further erode his kingship. He was afraid of his men. Driven by fear, he disobeyed God.

Fear and faithlessness

Fear is a remarkable motivator. It leads people to disobedience and faithlessness. It subverts our highest aspirations and makes hypocrites of many. We may have promised ourselves that we would be faithful, but fear robs us of commitments and takes the reward that might have been ours.

Let's consider an earlier time in Israel's history, recorded in Numbers 13 and 14. Israel, through the strong hand of God, had been delivered from Egyptian slavery and for the next two years they live in the Sinai Desert. There, at Mount Sanai, they learn the Ten Commandments and the laws of holy living. They build a tabernacle, learn about acceptable sacrifices to bring to God, what constituted appropriate worship, that forgiveness came only through the shedding of blood and that their God was holy. It was at the foot of Mount Sanai that the foundation of the nation of Israel was laid.

But then came the time to leave the Holy Mountain and move to the Promised Land. They knew battles lay before them, but how could they fear this? After all, the God they followed had already shown them his faithfulness by devastating their oppressors, Egypt, through a series of plagues. Further, when they fled He had parted the Red Sea and drowned the mighty Egyptian army's charioteers. If God was for them, who could be against them?

Leaving Mount Sinai, they arrived in short order at a place called Kadesh Barnea, on the edge of the Promised Land. Moses assigned twelve men to spy out the land and report back on the geography, fortifications and produce. When the spies return they announce that the land was indeed flowing with milk and honey—meaning it was fertile and capable of sustaining a large population. It was everything God had promised.

Numbers 13:27–28 records some of the spies' comments:

> We came to the land to which you sent us. It flows with milk and honey, and this is its fruit. However, the people who dwell in the land are strong, and the cities are fortified and very large. And besides, we saw the descendants of Anak there.

Who were these descendants of Anak? The Book of Deuteronomy indicates they were tall people and, for this reason alone, formidable opponents. But the spies took their thoughts one step further and gave in to their deepest fears, making them jump to conclusions. Numbers 13:33 records them as saying:

> And there we saw the Nephilim [the sons of Anak, who come from the Nephilim], and we seemed to ourselves like grasshoppers, and so we seemed to them.

The spies connected dots that should not have been connected: they thought the tall Anakites were direct descendants of the Nephilim, a powerful race of warriors mentioned in Genesis 6:4 who lived before Noah's days, when the violence on earth was so great that a universal flood was necessary to cleanse the world. The Nephilim, the mighty men of old, were so powerful that no one could stand against them.

Now, the spies should have known that all the Nephilim were killed in the flood, but instead they reported falsely that the greatest and most cruel race in human history was residing in the Promised Land.

Numbers 14 tells us that, when the people of Israel heard this, a cry went through the camp. Level-headed people should have cautioned the growing panic, saying, "This makes no sense at all. You are allowing your fears to rule you," but they did not. They lost both reason and faith and did not trust in God, who had brought them out of Egypt and fought for them along the way. Numbers 14:1 says, "Then all the congregation raised a loud cry, and the people wept that night."

That is a gracious way of putting it. I have no doubt people were shrieking with fear. Rumours began to spread as fear took hold of the population. Soon they were savagely blaming God for a crisis that did not exist. Numbers 14:3 tells us that they asked:

> Why is the LORD bringing us into this land, to fall by the sword? Our wives and our little ones will become prey. Would it not be better for us to go back to Egypt?

As in the case of King Saul, this moment of fear was pivotal. Because of their lack of faith and trust God set His face against that community, condemning them to wander around in circles in the wilderness for the next thirty-eight years until the entire generation who were over twenty years of age at that time would be dead. But the little ones whom they imagined would fall by the sword in the Promised Land would be the very ones who would inherit it.

Do not fear!

Fear is a strange thing. It paralyzes people, blinds them. It robs them of joy. It kills faith. It is no wonder there are numerous occasions when the Bible advises, "Do not fear." For example, after their father Jacob died, Joseph's brothers were fearful that Joseph would enact revenge upon them.

They asked, "What if Joseph hasn't really forgiven us? Perhaps the brother we wronged was only showing kindness so he could punish us after our father died? What if his benevolence was simply patience as he waited to get even? What if he believes revenge is a dish best served cold?"

In panic, they invent a lie. "Before dad died," they said, "he told us to tell you to forgive us," though nothing of the kind had been said by the dying man.

Joseph saw that they thought he might be vindictive and calmed them, saying, "Do not fear. Am I in the place of God?" meaning, "You're fearing the wrong person. You should be fearing God, not me."

Many years after Joseph, when the king of the Amorites made a concerted effort to counterattack the advances made by Joshua, the Lord spoke to Joshua, and said, "Do not fear them, for I have given them into your hands" (Joshua 10:8).

In Matthew 10:28, Jesus says, "Do not fear those who kill the body but cannot kill the soul."

And in Revelation 2:10, Jesus tells the church in Smyrna, "Do not fear what you are about to suffer."

Do not fear. Do not fear. Do not fear. God repeats it. It is essential to our faith. But think of how often we allow our fears to dominate us. I know of many people who are afraid of cancer. Within the church there are people who are afraid of giving generously lest they impoverish themselves, people who feel called into mission work but draw back because they think it might be too difficult. How many people fail to accept a challenge because they fear what might lie ahead of them? Our fears excite our imaginations, and fears are innumerable. Humans fear many things, including disease, love, lack of love and fear of failure. The list is literally endless.

The fear of people

At the top of the list for many is the fear of public speaking—including me! When I first started preaching I used to dream I was standing in the pulpit and had forgotten to put my pants on. I think I was afraid to be discovered spiritually and intellectually naked. I was afraid people would expose me for the empty fraud I was afraid I might be. I often wondered what a professional therapist might have said if I had revealed those dreams.

As unrealistic as some fears are, one that dominates is the fear of people. And to be honest, this is not entirely unrealistic. We have an enormous capacity to hurt others, and we are all aware of this. In high school we fear that the cool kids will make fun of us. As we grow older we fear we will be victims of slander. We may fear standing up to a bully. I have known pastors who are afraid to stand up to a power player in the church. They reason their employment is at stake, and it often is.

I have even known pastors who seek the presence of God more robustly than most other people who are afraid for their jobs within the political structures of their churches!

Fear can paralyze us so badly that it prevents us from trusting God. It can cause people to hide their gifts out of fear of criticism. It can frighten away good intentions. It can lead to sin. But can the doctrine of God's providential care over all things lead us out of the valley of fear?

Providence grows courage

The doctrine of Providence is not a theoretical belief in a theological proposition. It is a way to live without the crushing burden of our fears overwhelming us. Providence is meant to be believed and applied. No area of life is to remain outside of faith in a God who works in all things. For if God determines what shall be, loves His people and has promised that all things will work together for His glory and our long-term good, what remains of fear? Is fear not banished?

What do you fear? Poverty or want? Has God not promised to sustain you? Philippians 4:19 says, "And my God will supply every need of yours according to his riches in glory in Christ Jesus."

And if that promise were not enough, remember that the one who created you has determined all your days so that you might know the best possible eternity.

Do you fear death? Romans 8:35 tells us: "Who shall separate us from the love of Christ? Shall tribulation, or distress, or persecution, or famine, or nakedness, or danger, or sword?"

The answer to this is an overwhelming NO! None of these things can separate us from Christ, from the resurrection and the eternity He has prepared for us. Furthermore, if famine, nakedness, danger or the sword lie before us, God has willed these things because of His relentless love for us. The end of these matters will serve our eternal good. These things will not devastate us.

Providence and the fear of great cultural change

Let's apply what we have learned about fear to a contemporary local situation. I am speaking about the unique circumstances that are occurring in my country, Canada. All over the world we are witnessing people movement on a scale that has never been seen before, as refugees leave their homelands looking for safety. Furthermore, the low birthrate in the Western world has necessitated that Western countries look for immigrants, and so we have opened our borders to the world. This has created a cultural melting pot and irrevocably changed some of the old traditions of the past. The racial mix in my country is rapidly changing and will never be the same.

Some are deeply afraid of these changes. For some, this fear arises from a basic and ugly impulse to fear and despise people who do not share skin colour or racial background. This is called racism. But not all who fear the current changes are racist. Some fear the changing cultural values that the current influx of immigrants brings. There is a worry that any country can absorb only a certain number of immigrants and acculturate them. When the mass of immigrants is higher than can be absorbed, will not the basic fabric of our culture simply break? Will either chaos or a complete cultural shift be the result? That shift might be away from the kind of western liberal democracy we have come to know. What if this launches into the kind of violence that has become so dominant around the world? Some people fear.

I am not addressing what our policies should be. I leave that discussion to others. Governments have an obligation to address these matters. In a democracy, citizens have the right to address these matters. I am, however, speaking about the Providence of God and his meticulous sovereignty around all things. I am also speaking to the issue of the reaction of fear. Why should we fear? Should we not replace fear with a confidence that God does all things for His glory and the long-term good of those who love Him?

Sadly, some Christians are deeply afraid of immigration and, instead of seeing it as an opportunity to share the Gospel with people around the world who are now brought to their shores, they see it as a threat. How does the doctrine of Providence change our outlook? Let's affirm God's Providence regarding where it is that people live. While addressing the philosophers in Athens, Paul makes a remarkable statement that informs us in the present moment. In Acts 17:26, it says, "And He made from one man every nation of mankind to live on all the face of the earth, having determined allotted periods and the boundaries of their dwelling place."

Paul said that God determined both the boundaries of the nations as well as the time periods in which they would live within those boundaries. From the biblical narrative, we need to remember where the divisions of people into various races and cultures comes from. According to Genesis, the division of humanity came after the incident of the Tower of Babel. Before the flood the earth had but one culture, and had also become intolerably evil. God destroyed that world.

Shortly after the flood, as human civilization flourished again, human ingenuity leaped forward dramatically. But so also did human evil. God then separated out humanity, creating various and competing cultures. This prevented the ultimate human super society from developing. It limited evil through the restraints imposed upon them by competing nations. This was God's doing. But God also determined the length of each people group in history. As an easy example of this, one need only to ask what has become of the Moabites, the Ammonites, the Jebusites and the Girgashites. They existed within their time dimensions and are no more. However, other nations, such as the Syrians and Persians, still exist. God determines different things for different nations.

Let's bring this discussion into the present time. It is possible that we are now seeing Western liberal democracies not only changed, but brought to an end. We can't know if this is so, but it is certainly possible. God knows. But if this is so, it is God's doing. After all, it is the Western world that has led the movement away from God toward entrenched atheism. It is the Western world that has failed to produce children to replace itself. God may be decreeing that the West will fall as some ancient peoples who no longer exist. We can't know if such a time is upon us. But in Providence, God has decreed these matters.

But Paul is not done. In Acts 17:26, he says that God determines the allotted periods and boundaries during which nations and cultures exist. Further, in verse 27 he adds that he does this so that in due time all nations and civilizations are given the opportunity to seek God. I think one would have to be blind not to notice that the centre of global Christianity has moved from the West to the global South and certain places in the Asian world. The Gospel is growing in places where there was no Gospel growth before. All of this reflects God's intention that his future Kingdom be made up of people from every language, people group and racial characteristics. God delights in this.

I make no claim to be a missiologist, but I think one would have to be blind not to notice that we are living in a day of historic and seismic shifts in regard to the Christian faith. This is God's doing! Furthermore, there can be no doubt that Western values, however one defines them, have been corrosive to the Christian faith, despite that many of us pray the Lord will send a revival.

What is God doing? The birth rate in secular Western democracies is in full decline. Marriage is delayed and frequently abandoned utterly. Living together out of wedlock is the norm. Marriage, sexual expression and gender identity have been redefined. Abortion is commonplace. The nuclear family is denigrated. Children are not cherished and valued. Money and self-expression are more important than family and community. Deep and profound surrender to Christ as Lord is hard under this siege of values. Many of us pray that God will intervene.

Meanwhile, people of vastly different cultures and religions come to our door. Many of these people are open to the Gospel. They come from cultures where it is normal to speak about God. They are curious about the Christian faith and eager to learn from Christian people who want to share the Gospel. So instead of mourning the death of a culture that seems destined to die, should we not consider that if the West does not seek the Gospel, God will give these lands to those who do? If God is glorified, and the Gospel moves forward at the collapse of Western lifestyle and ways, then may it be so. We want the eternal Kingdom, not the substandard values and godlessness of this culture.

I regularly pray for two things.

First, I pray that God will awaken the Church in the West from its lethargy and fear; that we seize the opportunity given by God to share the Gospel with immigrants; and that, in cultures where conversion to Christianity results in people being alienated from family, that new immigrant converts find themselves enfolded in a new family of faith that sustains them.

Second, I pray that God might open the hearts of the many immigrants who come to the West to the Gospel in this land.

I am confident the grand historic events that are occurring are ordained and sustained by God so that men and women seek Him. I pray that God's people are not paralyzed by fear but respond with understanding that God is demonstrating His Providence over all things. He is determined to glorify himself through the Gospel and salvation of a vast company. Revelation 7:9-10 says:

> After this I looked, and behold, a great multitude that no one could number, from every nation, from all tribes and peoples and languages, standing before the throne and before the Lamb, clothed in white robes, with palm branches in their hands, and crying out with a loud voice, "Salvation belongs to our God who sits on the throne, and to the Lamb!"

A healthy belief in the Providence of God affects how we see world events. Of course, that doesn't mean hard times might not lie ahead; it seems every advance of the Gospel is accompanied by suffering. But if you are with me in this—if you believe God rules and these days are arranged as he meant to arrange them—then does that not remove fear and replace it with willingness to ask God what these days mean? Should we not also ask what we must do in these days? Should we not be actively building churches that reach the many who are, by God's designs, being brought to our shores?

Whenever we apply the doctrine of Providence, we replace fear with spiritual insight and gain a heart for the peoples of the world. When we face personal crisis we will not fear. Instead of being overwhelmed by darkness, we can proclaim, "Our God rules," and know that it is so.

How about you? Has the doctrine of God's Providence led you to approach life with enthusiasm and confidence? Or have you not yet learned how the truths of scripture make a difference to the way you live your life. Perhaps you might want to ask God to help you believe those things that he has declared to be true.

CHAPTER 13

Providence Says, "Be Joyful"

French Philosopher Blaise Pascal had a great deal to say about happiness:

> All men seek happiness. This is without exception.
> Whatever different means they employ, they all tend to
> this end. The cause of some going to war, and of others
> avoiding it, is the same desire in both, attended with
> different views. The will never takes the least step but
> to this object. This is the motive of every action of every
> man, even those who hang themselves.[15]

The idea that the human will never acts without happiness in mind is a strange thought to some. But we have already spoken about human freedom. Freedom consists in doing what we want. This, as we saw, is a matter of the affections, or the strong inclinations of the soul. We are motivated by the things that please us. We want the things that we believe will bring us happiness.

Let's not tease out a distinction between happiness and joy; instead, let's say that both words mean being satisfied and content. On that matter, I think Pascal is right when he says that even those who make great sacrifices do so for the sake of happiness. The desire for greater good attracts many with the reward of joy. Joy is the motivation for all

---

[15]   Pascal, Blaise, 1623-1662. Pascal's Pensées. New York: E.P. Dutton, 1958.

human actions; hence, from that perspective there is little distinction to be made between happiness and joy.

Pascal asks, "How can it be that if all people are motivated by happiness, that people so rarely attain it?"

And further:

> And yet after such a great number of years, no one without faith has reached the point to which all continually look. *All complain,* princes and subjects, noblemen and commoners, old and young, strong and weak, learned and ignorant, healthy and sick, of all countries, all times, all ages, and all conditions.[16]

Pascal's words ring true. Listen to people talk and you soon hear them complaining. We don't like the weather. We don't like the politicians. We don't like our relatives. We don't like our work colleagues or our boss. We don't like the idiots on the road during our daily commute. We think the medical system has failed us. People even complain on car bumper stickers and on T-shirts, displaying slogans that read I'D RATHER BE FISHING or I'D RATHER BE GOLFING, making it clear to the world that whatever activity they are doing, it is not as satisfying as they would like. There is an ideal far more satisfying than their present reality. Hence, they are complaining.

But Pascal gives an exception. No one "without faith" has reached that goal to which everyone strives. Pascal believes that without faith we continually complain. Furthermore, Pascal thinks that this incessant complaining doesn't confine itself to one class of people. Both princes and commoners engage in the very same thing. Both are unhappy. But does Pascal think that the person of faith can reach the goal of happiness? Is he right? For if faith in Christ can achieve the goal of joy, it is a most valuable thing indeed.

This chapter will address this vital question. Pascal continues:

> A trial so long, so continuous, and so uniform should certainly convince us of our inability to reach the

---

[16] Ibid

good by our own efforts . . . What is it then that this
desire and this inability to proclaim to us, but that
there was once in man a true happiness of which there
now remains to him only; the mark and empty trace,
which he in vain tries to fill from all his surroundings,
seeking from things absent the help he does not obtain
in things present? But these are all inadequate, because
the infinite abyss can only be filled by an infinite and
immutable Object, that is to say, only by God Himself.[17]

Well said! Let's see if we can break down Pascal's thoughts into
smaller units to help us understand. Pascal says the unhappiness of
all people is long and enduring, using the words "continuous" and
"uniform." He means that the human experience has always been
uniform, or that it has been unchanging through the ages. That is a
deep dissatisfaction that we all know, and it never seems to go away.
What we seek most is always absent.

Why is that? Pascal's answer is that an infinite abyss exists within
us. Others have called this "a God-shaped vacuum." Pascal speaks of
what humans had before the fall, which has now been lost. In vain
we try to fill the abyss of our discontented spirits in a multitude of
ways, casting around for things that might take away the sting of our
disappointments. We tell ourselves that if we could only find the right
wife or husband, we'd be happy; if we only had more money, we'd be
happy; if we could find the right job, where we were properly respected,
we'd be happy. If only people would recognize the contributions we
have made. If we could only get into medical school. If I could only find
the ideal job that suited my innate talents. If I could only have enough
money that I wouldn't need a job. If only we could achieve fame and
revel in the applause of others. But this lack of joy was never intended
to be filled by that which we eagerly pursue. After all, the vacuum is
God-shaped.

[17]   Ibid

Joy is a Christian virtue

One of the key Christian virtues is joy. Others are gratitude, praise and thankfulness. Psalm 107:1 says, "Oh, give thanks to the LORD, for he is good, for his steadfast love endures forever!"

And then, as if this were not enough, verse 2 adds, "Let the redeemed of the LORD say so."

Giving thanks to God is a command. 1 Thessalonians 5:18 reinforces this, commanding us: "Give thanks in all circumstances."

We should all make a practice of continually thanking God regardless of the circumstances in which we find ourselves. Why? Because it is necessary for us to discover that the only enduring joy is found in the beauty of God Himself. We should be thankful not only because He providentially arranges all our lives, but for the Lord Himself. He is the object of our greatest joy!

As well as the joy of knowing Him who is the object and source of all joy, God also brings benefits into every believer's life. In Psalm 16:6–11, we are told:

> The lines have fallen for me in pleasant places; indeed, I have a beautiful inheritance.
> I bless the Lord who gives me counsel; in the night also, my heart instructs me.
> I have set the Lord always before me; because He is at my right hand, I shall not be shaken.
> Therefore, my heart is glad, and my whole being rejoices; my flesh also dwells secure. For you will not abandon my soul to Sheol, or let your holy one see corruption.
> You make known to me the path of life; in your presence there is fullness of joy; at your right hand are pleasures forevermore.

Did you notice how skillfully David puts together his feelings about both the kindness God brings into his life, and the joy of being in a relationship with God? David starts with the comment "the lines have fallen for me in pleasant places." What he means is that his life has turned out to his satisfaction, for which he is grateful. This is a great statement on David's faith, for he led a life of turmoil as well as victory. After all, for years he was hunted by Saul, and in the latter days of his life his family life descended into turmoil that led to civil war. But to David, the lines fell in some good places, and from his perspective he is satisfied. To the cynic, this seems almost unimaginable. Surely things would have been better had David not suffered the sorrows along with the victories.

But it all depends on perspective. And perspective is exactly what David is talking about. Psalm 16 begins with the words: "Preserve me, O God, for in you I take refuge."

That David needs a place of refuge tells us he is writing in a time of crisis. In Verse 4 he remarks that the sorrows of those who run after another god shall multiply, but for him and those who do not the lines fall in pleasant places. With these words he is acknowledging that God arranges matters in his life so that they result in the best possible outcome. David remarks that God gives him counsel through the difficult days he is facing, and that God never abandons him. That alone is reason enough for joy. David knows the pleasure he finds in God supersedes all life's disappointments.

C.S. Lewis, like Blaise Pascal, had a great deal to say about joy:

> If we consider the unblushing promises of reward and the staggering nature of the rewards promised in the Gospels, it would seem that our Lord finds our desires not too strong, but too weak. We are half-hearted creatures, fooling around with drink and sex and ambition when infinite joy is offered us, like an ignorant child who wants to go on making mud pies in a slum because he cannot imagine what is meant by the offer of a holiday at the sea. We are far too easily pleased.[18]

Lewis rightly places his insightful finger on a key issue. How is it that we choose lesser pleasures that only thrill the soul for a brief moment instead of the great reward of knowing God? Or, in Lewis's words, how is it we prefer mud pies in a slum to a holiday by the sea?

---

[18]   Lewis, C. S. *The Weight of Glory*. HarperOne, 2015.

Earthly delights do give pleasures, but they are fleeting. These lesser pleasures leave the soul with remorse, pain and unfulfilled expectation, whereas the staggering eternal rewards of God leave us with no regret, only great joy. There must be a secret as to why we abandon the greater for the sake of the lesser.

Why believers in Jesus complain

In 1 Timothy 4:4-5, Paul says, "For everything created by God is good, and nothing is to be rejected if it is received with thanksgiving, for it is made holy by the word of God and prayer."

Paul is writing against those who create rules that forbid marriage and require the abstinence of certain foods to demonstrate their holiness. In contrast, Paul counsels believers to live joyfully in the world. "Marry if you want," he says, "provided you do so in the Lord. Eat whatever is set before you, provided you give thanks, for what you have is from God."

A healthy doctrine of creation tells us that creation is good. We should enjoy this world, for it was not only created *by* God, but *for* Him. Creation demonstrates the glory of God. God Himself finds delight in what He has made. As we have learned, God sustains this world at each moment. The world we enjoy has been willed to continue by Him who finds delight in it. Why then shouldn't we also? God, who is the source of all joy, invites us to revel in the beauty of the world He has created and to tell Him we love it and are satisfied in His works.

Yet still we complain, and I am convinced it is because we doubt the doctrine of Providence. We doubt that God arranged all things for His glory and our long-term good. Instead, we wonder if we are missing something that might bring us greater joy and, if misfortune strikes, we doubt that God's hand was in it, mistakenly believing our painful experiences can't be part of a joyful outcome. Like Eve in the garden, we believe that God is withholding something from us. Do you remember the temptation of the serpent? "God knows that when you eat, you will be like God." That is, like Eve, we believe that something is being withheld from us. Like Israel in the desert, we murmur and complain.

Why do we suspect there is greater joy in breaking God's commandments than in keeping them? Do we think we will miss something? Do we think fulfilling immediate desires will serve us better than reveling in God's beauty? Is our problem our faith? Do we not trust that the one who created us loves us enough to fill us with eternal joy?

The strategy of deliberate thankfulness

I asked some of my colleagues to tell me about things for which we should be thankful but we mostly complain about. One of my female colleagues immediately said, "Oh, that happens most often in the grocery store."

I was puzzled. "How so?" I asked.

She told me that complaints in the grocery store are monumental. "The lineups are too long. Why isn't the lineup of fifteen items or less open? And when it is open, why do they allow people into that lineup when they have more than fifteen items in their cart? Why are you always out of Ambrosia apples?" In Canada, people complain that the French translation is facing forward; in Quebec and New Brunswick it's the English side that is appearing. And what's with the wobbly wheels on some of the carts? I bet it's the government's fault!

Think of how different those experiences could be if we were given the perspective of the kind providence of God. The lineups are long, and you give thanks to God that so many people are able both to afford food and to find it in abundance! The French side of the package is sticking out so you remind yourself of the grace of a country in which two historic enemies found peace and a way to coexist. The wheels on your shopping cart do wobble, but you are reminded that you are able to afford so much food that it requires a wheeled cart to get it out of the store and into your car. It may require quite a walk to get from your car to the store, but amazingly you have a car that will soon be filled with food for you and your family.

All our responses depend on perspective. If God is arranging all things for His glory and our long-term good, we would do well to actively examine all the mundane things, including our experience in the grocery store. Isn't it true that if we took the time, we would see God's kindness in the grocery store? Furthermore, no matter how disorganized that store might be, the food is safe to consume. What an amazing blessing!

I add a trivial example about thanklessness and unhappiness. I will not soon forget what happened in my city some years ago. We had so much rain that silt from the hillsides washed into our reservoirs, leaving the water cloudy. We were advised to boil all drinking water and pass it through a coffee filter. Predictably, the local grocery store experienced a high demand for bottled drinking water, so they brought loaded pallets of the stuff and set them in the middle of the floor. The bottles quickly disappeared, and the last few left for the day were specially prized. Amazingly, though all anyone had to do to ensure their water was safe was to boil it, fistfights occurred over these last bottles of water. Fistfights! And blood was spilled. Instead of thankfulness for the abundance of safe drinking water, there was rage and anger!

These are evils of the wealthy who are blessed with abundance. I have been to many parts of the world where drinkable water is always lacking. Rather than fistfights, thanks and gratitude should have been in order at the grocery store on that day. Instead, fear reigned. People failed to consider the abundance that comes from God.

What has this to do with Providence? Everything. Once we embrace God's Providence, we find that nothing happens by accident. Not only is there no bad luck, there is no luck at all. The universe is not governed by fate or a bad alignment of the stars. Nothing just *happens*. Instead, all things are arranged by the providential hand of God, for his glory and the long-term good of those he has chosen, including the amount of rain we get and the silt that washes into the watershed. Once we embrace how God wisely arranges all things in our lives, we gain confidence in discovering how to grow in holiness, lean upon His grace and consider the needs of others before our own.

But does Providence really apply to all things, like the grocery clerk who always stocks the shelves with the French side out, or the traffic light that turns yellow just when you get there, or the person who cut you off in traffic? And what about when we lose our job, our health, our loved ones? Are we to consider *all* things as coming from the hand of God who creates and sustains? Can we really be thankful in all things?

Thankfulness from the Book of Philippians

Let's consider a test case on how to be thankful from the Book of Philippians. Philippians was written by Paul while he was in prison in Rome, awaiting trial before Caesar's tribunal. The events that led to Paul's imprisonment were, from one perspective, a tragedy. Paul had gone to Jerusalem to bring the proceeds of an offering to help the needy Christians there. While in Jerusalem a false rumour was traded about, saying that Paul had brought Trophimus, an Ephesian, a gentile, into the Jewish temple. It wasn't true, but it sent the city into an uproar. Indeed, Paul would have been killed in the ensuing riot had not a Roman tribune intervened and saved his life.

Paul was put under guard, but a group of forty Jewish extremists conspired to assassinate him, and so he was moved from Jerusalem to the city of Caesarea, where the Romans had their garrison. But in truth Paul was in prison for something he had not done, and there he stayed for two years—without a trial! The governor was keeping Paul in prison to appease the Jewish extremists. It was outrageous.

Finally, Paul took the only legal avenue open to him. Since he had Roman citizenship, he appealed to Caesar. However, shortly after he made this appeal, King Agrippa and the governor met. Agrippa informed the governor that had Paul not appealed to Caesar, he could have been released immediately. One wonders if Paul, hearing of this, may have concluded he had acted too hastily in making his appeal. Perhaps, he might have thought, he had made a mistake.

One interpretation of these events might be that this was an unfortunate turn of events. What bad luck! Another interpretation might be to say that had Paul listened more closely to God's leading, or been more patient, things would not have turned out this way. But now, in consequence of his apparent bad decision, the indeterminate imprisonment in Caesarea was about to turn into imprisonment in Rome awaiting Caesar's tribunal. There Paul would face the possibility of being found guilty of sedition against the emperor. A trial would ensue. If found innocent he would be released. If found guilty he would immediately be executed. And all this because of a series of unfounded rumours, followed by a city-wide riot in Jerusalem.

In the face of these events, Paul might have complained. Who would blame him for such a response? After all, if people would just check the facts before believing rumours, so much evil could be avoided. But that didn't happen. People who heard the rumours believed them, putting Paul in a terrible predicament. Paul might also have complained, "If the Roman authorities in Caesarea had taken just, courageous action and released me, my life wouldn't be on trial." If Paul had allowed a bitter experience to persist he might even have levelled his complaints at God. Had God intervened this matter would not have happened. How could God stand idly by and allow evil men to have their way and stop this most effective missionary from doing his work?

The book of Philippians is written while Paul was imprisoned in Rome and awaiting his trial. The church of Philippi was in northern Greece. Paul had planted that church years earlier. Since that time they had become his most faithful partner in ministry, and when they heard of his imprisonment they raised money to take care of his physical needs. They entrusted the money to a deacon named Epaphroditus, who risked his life to travel from Greece to Rome. While he was there, Epaphroditus was also required to bring news home to the church in Philippi. Everyone wanted to know how Paul was doing. Was he discouraged? Was he fearful? Did he believe his work was over? Was the partnership between Paul and the Philippian church also now over? What did the future hold? How was the church to pray for Paul?

Paul sent a letter back with Epaphroditus. That letter is now the biblical Book of Philippians. And what does it say? Paul explains his situation: "I have been chained daily to a Roman guard. But he is not just any guard. I am chained to a member of the imperial guard, the praetorium. This is the most elite military force in the city. They are also the guards that are responsible for the emperor's safety. God has given me an opportunity to share the Gospel with these elite men. And they have been talking. Consequently, all of Caesar's household is talking about Jesus. Had it not been for my imprisonment, we would never have been able to bring the Gospel message into the heart of the Roman Empire!"

But that is not all of the good things that had come from his Roman imprisonment. The Christian Church in Rome, which had for some time been intimidated by the city's imperial might, was seeing Paul's boldness for the Gospel. And they were inspired! That Church was now redoubling their efforts to share the Gospel of Jesus in the world. But there were even more benefits that flowed from Paul's imprisonment. In a short period Paul would be standing before Caesar's tribunal. He would then be asked to share the message he had been preaching everywhere. No doubt they would be ascertaining if his activity was illegal. But from Paul's perspective this was an opportunity to share the saving news of Jesus with the most powerful judiciary in the world.

The point to be learned from Philippians is profound. Were it not for a series of rumours begun by hateful people in Jerusalem, the opportunities to boldly preach in Rome would never have occurred. How could Paul complain about evil men spreading false rumours, when the good and faithful God ordained that this event would trigger others that would lead to the advancement of the Gospel throughout the Roman Empire and beyond?

In Philippians 1:18, Paul says, "In that I rejoice. Yes, and I will rejoice."

Paul was saying that he was rejoicing because of the good his imprisonment had brought. He says that he will rejoice in the future when he is given the opportunity to testify before Caesar's tribunal. His joy knows no bounds. Rather than feeling angry at the injustice he had experienced, Paul was able to see beyond it to the gracious God who did all things for Paul's good and for His glory. Philippians is testimony that thankfulness pervades all things, if only we see the sovereign hand of God.

"If God be for us . . ."

We began this chapter by noting that all people are motivated to seek happiness, but happiness is fleeting. Pascal had noticed a universal phenomenon: all people complain. This is because the events in our lives never turn out in the way we had imagined they should have. We might add to this thought that a great many people nurse grudges and harbour feelings of deep betrayal and bitterness. They believe they deserve better.

But the joy for which humans have been created is different. This joy begins by assuming the truth of God's kind Providence. From there we look for God's hand in all circumstances. And if we are observant, and if we look carefully, we will be overjoyed in the ways of God.

Paul said, "In that I rejoice. Yes, and I will rejoice." May we never say, "In that I complain. Yes, and I will complain."

CHAPTER 14

Providence Says, "Live by Faith"

Years ago I had a marvelous afternoon with a local university professor. We had never met, but he contacted my office to make an appointment with me. He told me he needed to satisfy his intellectual curiosity about Christianity and, since he had no background in the Christian faith, he thought it would be interesting to talk to a Christian pastor. He asked me, "Would you be interested in answering some of my questions?"

I told him, "That is what I do for a living. I talk to people about the Christian faith in any number of forums, and a personal interview is just fine with me."

We spent several hours together. It was a delightful time. Near the beginning of our conversation, he said, "I assume you believe in faith."

I said, "I don't believe in faith. I believe in God."

He looked confused and asked me to explain. He said, "I thought the reason for believing in God was because one believed in faith as a way of seeing reality."

I smiled. The man was thoughtful. I liked him immediately. I told him, "In my estimation, faith and belief are synonyms. If I were to ask you if you believe in the scientific method, would you interpret the emphasis of my question to be on the matter of believing or on the veracity of the scientific method?" He and I both knew the answer. "In the same way," I said, "it is the content of belief in God that directs my faith. That there is a God who has revealed Himself in scripture is the essential question. That I believe in Him follows from the truth of His existence."

He hesitated for a moment. He told me he could see my point, but he was interested in a different line of thought. For him, the principal question remained the definition of faith. He told me his understanding of Christian faith is the belief in those things for which there is no empirical evidence. Did I agree? Was faith a confidence in those things which could never be proven?

"Where did you get such a definition of faith?" I asked him.

He told me that as a rule, that is how he had understood the term. Furthermore, it was a common assumption among his university colleagues. I told him that in my estimation *all* human beings believed in certain unprovable assumptions. We both believed that our five senses are accurately communicating to our brains what is really present in the natural world. We assume it, even while we can't prove it. But in my case, I also believed in things that were not accessible to my five senses. But while I readily admitted to this, this did not answer the question of *why* I believed in these things. But to answer the initial question plainly, the answer was a firm no. I do not think the definition of faith is the belief in things for which there was no evidence. I think people who believe in the tooth fairy, the sasquatch and Santa Claus are not people of faith. There is a world of difference between faith and gullibility, or between faith and prejudice.

He engaged immediately. "So," he said, "we are both driven by evidence?"

"Yes," I agreed. "Although what constitutes trustworthy evidence might be quite different between the two of us."

On we went until we were talking about the cross, the resurrection and why I not only believed in these things but staked my entire life on them. We talked about how the cross constituted the only hope for forgiveness for humanity's transgressions of God's laws; we even spoke briefly of the judgment to come. All in all, the conversation was direct, challenging and respectful. It really was the kind of conversation I wish I could have every day.

Faith in an unfailing person

I have reflected on that conversation since. I wonder how many people think of faith in the way this professor thought of it, that it is a matter of believing in things for which there is no evidence. I suppose there are many people who think it doesn't matter what you believe, just that you believe with sincerity. Others simply see faith as a set of guiding principles.

In contrast, biblical faith is grounded in the person of the one true God. The very start of genuine faith is the firm conviction that the God of the Bible exists. I say it that way so that I leave no room for idolatry. Idolatry begins with human conceptions of God. Biblical faith begins with God's revelation of himself. The first is grounded in human contrivance, the second in God's self-disclosure. There is a world of difference between these two. The first emphasizes faith, the second emphasizes the object of our faith.

Biblical faith never asks us to *conceive* of God; indeed, it renounces such an approach. Biblical faith is *revelational*. If the Eternal One did not condescend to speak to us in ways in which we can understand, we would not know Him. We might know something of God's eternal nature and power from what we observe in creation. We would know that, because the Creator made a world that sustains us, we owe Him a debt of gratitude. But we would not know if the Creator is cruel or loving because, while we see his bountiful care, we also see death and suffering. We might, as the Greeks and Romans did, conceive of him as fickle—he provides for us but also curses us.

Biblical faith rests in two things.

First, in the revelation of God's self-disclosure provided for us in scripture.

Second, it trusts that God is love. After all, did He not send His Son into the world to be our Saviour? Is it not reasonable, then, that we entrust our lives to Him, resting in His wisdom rather than our own?

Defining faith

What difference does a healthy biblical view of God's Providence mean in everyday life? God's loving Providence provides the groundwork for living life with courage and joy. But how does Providence provide the groundwork of faith? And is it possible that those who believe in God's Providence have an enlarged capacity to trust God?

I began to define faith by recreating my conversation with the university professor who visited me. This man had reason to be confused about what faith means. Even in the Christian faith, we have differing views. An aberrant movement within the church, the Word of Faith doctrine holds that faith is an impersonal force used by God Himself. Word of Faith teachers argue that we don't put our faith in God, but rather that we put our faith in faith. To them, as God spoke and the world came into existence, so we also speak, and cancer goes away or wealth appears. For these people, faith is very much like the force in Star Wars: if properly manipulated, it will do what we intend.

In my estimation, the Word of Faith movement can't properly be called Christian because Christians are called upon to trust God. For Christians, there is a vast difference between God and people. God is immortal, we are mortal. God is all powerful, we are limited in strength. God is all wise and all knowing, our knowing is limited and fallible. God's existence is non-contingent, meaning that He exists by necessity. Our existence is contingent, meaning that we exist due of factors outside of our control. God is Creator, we are creation. I could go on and on, but the point is that faith is trust in God, not in faith. We never trust in a faith we can conjure up through our efforts. Rather, the emphasis is on God.

Three aspects of biblical faith

The Bible gives us three different aspects of faith. The first involves knowing and believing a group of truths. Jude 3 gives us a very good definition:

> Beloved, although I was very eager to write to you about our common salvation, I found it necessary to write appealing to you to contend for the faith that was once for all delivered to the saints.

1. Faith as the content of truth

Notice here that in Jude 3 the word "faith" is not a verb, but a noun. Furthermore, it is a noun with an article in front of it—*the* faith. Jude says that it is necessary to contend for "the faith," so we must assume some were either attacking it, redefining it or adding to it. After all, Jude says the faith was given once for all.

When faith is used as a noun, it is used to define the corpus of Christian belief. Faith sets the stage for our doctrines. What is it we believe about the Bible? What do we believe about the nature of God? What is it we believe about Jesus and the meaning of the cross? What do we believe about the Bible's claim that Jesus is both fully God and fully man at the same time? What is the incarnation? What do we believe about salvation? Is Christ's death a substitutionary atonement? Yes, it is! What do we believe about angels and demons? What does it mean to be human? What is sin? What is the judgment? How are we forgiven? How do we grow in holiness? What is the meaning of baptism and the Lord's table? What do we believe about the end of history and the second coming of Jesus?

All these things are the content of our faith. They are what we might call propositional truths. Deny these truths and you deny the faith. And so it *does* matter what you believe. For if you are errant in your beliefs, you are outside of the faith. These things are not about how sincere you are, they are about whether you believe those truths which God has revealed concerning himself.

When it comes to the faith, we know that some of the revealed truths are primary, and others are secondary. That is not to say that some truths are less important; rather, it is to say that some truths are foundational while others build upon these foundational truths. Genuine Christians do not disagree on the foundational truths. All Christians around the world, regardless of location, culture or ethnic makeup, affirm these same truths. If we deny them, we deny our faith and inclusion in the Kingdom to come. This is the one faith, once and for all delivered to the saints.

Let me re-emphasize: you are not in the faith if you don't or can't affirm certain foundational propositions to be true. On this basis, no genuine Christian will ever say it doesn't matter what you believe as long as you are sincere and it makes you a better person. To say that is the very opposite of what we mean by faith. Faith has an object. That object is both God Himself and the essential truths concerning Himself that He revealed in the Bible.

2. Faith as the assurance of things hoped for

The second aspect of faith is inner conviction of the truths of the Bible relays. Hebrews 11:1 says, "Now faith is the assurance of things hoped for, the conviction of things not seen."

Two words catch our attention: assurance and conviction. Faith is an inner certitude that what we have been promised by God are not fables or empty promises, and while Christians may have moments to doubt, faith rests in the security that God is greater than those doubts.

There is an old musical stage play called *Oklahoma*. Its most famous song is "Oh, What a Beautiful Mornin'" that expresses the joyful faith of everything going our way. Is faith that beautiful feeling that everything is going to be okay? Or something else? For some people, faith *is* that beautiful feeling. They are glass-half-full people, the optimistic types. But when Hebrews speaks of assurance, note that the Greek word for assurance is *hypostasis*, or "confidence." This means that biblical faith is not grounded in wishful thinking or positivity. One can have a settled confidence that the things promised are to be counted on, despite one's disposition.

Hypostasis is used two more times in Hebrews. In chapter 1:3 we read of Jesus: "He is the radiance of the glory of God and the exact imprint of His nature."

The word translated as "nature" comes from *hypostasis*. In the context of Hebrews 1:3, it means that Jesus is identical in substance to God. To say that Jesus is the imprint of the nature of the Father is to say that what is essentially true of God is essentially true of Jesus. Therefore, we can take the word *hypostasis* to mean "essential nature" or "essence."

Let's go back to Hebrews 11:1. Faith, says the writer of Hebrews, is the essence, or the true nature, of what we hope for. That is, there is not a distinction to be made between what is hoped for and the things that are promised to us by God. The two things are the same. Faith is not a vague feeling that everything's going to turn out just right. Rather, it is an expectation of something which has been objectively promised by a faithful God.

We next find the word *hypostasis* in Hebrews 3:14: "For we have come to share in Christ, if indeed we hold our original confidence firm to the end."

Again, the word translated as "confidence" comes from *hypostasis*. "Holding our original confidence" refers to being so sure of Christ and his ability to do that which he has promised so that we respond appropriately. In the context of Hebrews, it means we never let go of Christ regardless of the difficulty of suffering we may be called to endure.

Now let's put this together. Faith is the essence of what we hope for, as well as the confidence in things hoped for. Faith seizes upon something hoped for, as if the confidence itself were a real essence or substance. It is as if the confidence we have is as substantive as the thing for which we hope. There are then, if you will, two realities. The first is the reality of what God has promised will occur in the future. The second is the inner confidence in the promise.

Let's restate that. There are two actualities here. One is the truth that at the last judgment those who have placed their hope in Christ will be exonerated of all their sins. They will enter the joy of their master. They will see God face to face and be welcomed into eternal dwellings. These things are genuine. The second actuality, equally genuine and equally profound, is the confidence that believers have in these things. So much confidence that it directs the nature of their lives.

Think of it this way. Let's say someone promises you a million dollars. You might say, "I hope he delivers, but who knows?" That's a hope, to be sure, but it is not a confident one. But let's say someone transfers a million dollars into your bank account. You go online and there it is! Now, you don't say that you hope the funds will be there when you need them. Rather, you now have confidence that when you require those funds they will be available. Until now you haven't touched the money and haven't spent it. But you have a *hypostasis*. You have a substance that reflects a genuine reality. And that is what faith is.

Remember that through scripture faith is defined as something given to us by God, not something we generate through our own efforts. John 6:65 records Jesus saying, "No one can come to me unless it is granted him by the Father."

Romans 12:3 also indicates that God gives each their own measure of faith. However we understand these passages, we know with certainty that in some mysterious fashion, every believer has a deep, settled conviction that is so real that it is not a matter of "I *choose* to believe." How can anyone choose such a depth of confidence? Rather, Christians have a unique certainty. They say, "I find in myself a deep, abiding confidence in God." At times they are amazed to find how deeply that confidence is held. For the sake of it they would gladly forsake all the earth has to give, for they know their God remains when it is the earth itself that is transitory.

And that, says the writer of Hebrews, is the definition of faith. It is a reality. It is a substance. It is a deep confidence that corresponds to things that have been promised by the Father. These things are difficult to explain to those who have never had faith. The person without faith may indeed hope the things revealed in scripture are true, but those who truly believe understand that their faith has substance.

We have looked at two aspects of faith. The first is the *content* of what we believe. The second is the *deep, abiding confidence* in what God has promised. We still must discuss the third aspect of faith, as well as discover how providence impacts our faith.

3. Faith is surrender

The third aspect of faith is surrender to Christ. It is the willingness to confess our sins to the one who calls us a sinner. When we first confess our sins, for the first time ever we say something in which we agree with God. God says we are sinners, and we agree.

Confessing our sins is an act of surrender to Christ as Lord. In Matthew 16:24–25, Jesus speaks about what it means to be his follower:

> Then Jesus told His disciples, "If anyone would come after me, let him deny himself and take up his cross and

follow me. For whoever would save his life will lose it, but whoever loses his life for my sake will find it."

Jesus called His disciples to abandon everything, to surrender what they might want for what He, their Lord, would want, which was to address Him as Lord and say, "Not my will, but yours be done." This is central to genuine faith.

Some object and argue that this definition goes too far. This, they say, is not *saving* faith; we must lower the bar. We are saved, they insist, when we believe Jesus died for our sins and trust Him with our salvation. Surrendering into the hands of Jesus is important, they tell us, but not necessary for salvation.

Are we indeed raising the bar too high? Not according to scripture. Consider Philippians 3:8b. Paul says, "For His sake I have suffered the loss of all things and count them as rubbish, in order that I may gain Christ."

Let's consider what Paul is communicating. In Paul's world, before his conversion he counted the value of things in a different way than he did after his conversion. Before conversion his status as a Jew counted, and Paul revelled in the fact that he was a Pharisee. Furthermore, he believed that his track record of blameless, legalistic righteousness under the law counted. These were not just of great value to him, but essential to his self-identity.

And then came his conversion, and those things that used to matter no longer did. In fact, he said he now counted the things he once revelled in as manure, and to revel in them seemed vile.

We might be tempted to say, "Good for Paul. He was an exceptional man. That is most inspiring." But this does him a disservice. In Paul's mind it was not possible to gain Christ if he did not suffer the loss of all other things. It was a binary decision: either he would gain and retain temporal things or he would lose it all and gain Christ instead. It was not possible to have both at the same time.

Let's continue. Paul further says in Philippians 3:8-9:

That I may gain Christ and be found in Him, not having a righteousness of my own that comes from the law, but that which comes through faith in Christ, the righteousness from God that depends on faith.

Here we find familiar language describing saving faith. We no longer trust in ourselves; rather, we trust in Christ for our salvation. And this is correct! Our righteousness is not our own. We do not say, as some do, "I am righteous!" Rather, we say that Christ is righteous, and that in some wonderful fashion Christ's righteous record has been credited to our account. We trust both in the merits of Christ's spotless life and in His substitutionary death. Our sins are paid for. His track record is applied to us. We don't hold trust in ourselves, but in Him. This is the Gospel.

And this is how we are justified by faith. Genuine faith involves believing both in God and in the content of God's revealed truth. The scripture tells us that Christ died for us. We respond by believing this truth. It is more than an intellectual recognition, it involves a deep, inner, settled conviction that Christ saved us through His sacrificial death on the cross.

In Philippians 3 Verse 10, after Paul tells us that he now trusts fully in Christ, he says, "That I may know Him and the power of His resurrection, and may share His sufferings, becoming like Him in His death."

Here we see a clear picture of Paul's changed value system. Everything he once thought was important now seems like rubbish to him. Indeed, the only thing that matters is Christ. Furthermore, Paul wants to be so identified with Christ that he wants to share in his sufferings.

Remember, Jesus said that for anyone to follow him they must deny themselves, pick up their cross and follow him. In Philippians, Paul declares that this is what he has done. He has turned from his past life and surrendered to Christ.

That experience of repentance and surrender is not limited to Paul. Among many Christians throughout the world, the surrender that is required is immediately felt. Some people, when they come to Christ, are thrown out of their families and thus their circumstances demand it be either Christ or their families.

I have a memory of an event in which one of my fellow pastors at the church I worked at was getting ready to baptize several people on a Sunday morning. The service had already begun and my colleague was in the back with the baptismal candidates, giving them last-minute instructions and praying with them.

As they waited to enter the sanctuary, one woman made a comment to my colleague. She said that when she came to Christ, her family was unsettled but willing to make peace with her conversion. However, they cautioned, "You can believe in Jesus, but if you ever decide to get baptized none of us will ever have dealings with you again."

My colleague was stunned. He had not known how momentous this event was for this woman. She was abandoning all she had ever loved for Christ. She had read Jesus's commands to pick up her cross and follow him, and to repent and be baptized. Because she believed and had faith it was necessary for her to surrender to the will of Christ. "Not my will but yours be done."

And what her family had threatened, they did. Several years after her baptism she saw her mother in a grocery store. She attempted to speak to her, but her mother turned her gaze from her and simply walked away. It is essential to invite people like this into Christian homes and graft them into church families. Many brothers and sisters have paid a staggering cost to embrace Christ. They have thought that Christ was the ultimate prize, and that all other things are nothing in comparison to him.

Faith and the doctrine of Providence

Genuine faith is so often misunderstood. It must be understood rightly before the connection between faith and the Providence of God can be made. Remember, God created and sustains all things for his glory and our long-term good. For some, following Jesus costs them everything, and so it is of great comfort to know these costs are not apart from his loving long-term care. Belief in Providence assures us that God has arranged every detail so that, in the eternal ages to come, our joy is maximized.

Paul said that momentary light afflictions are earning us eternal weight in glory. You and I can go through the afflictions our faith demands of us, knowing that they are orchestrated, designed and prepared for us in advance. It is necessary for people of faith to have their faith perfected by the sufferings Christ demands of us. A God of love demands that we pay a price.

Sometimes the cost is high. A few summers ago in Canada, the government mandated that, for any organization to receive summer job funding for their summer programs, the applicant must affirm the right of a woman to receive an abortion. This included all church groups and Christian organizations. There would be no government grants to Christian groups apart from an affirmation of the policy of abortion on demand.

A great many Christian ministries avail themselves of such government funds, something I think leads to temptation to compromise essential values. Nevertheless, in the providential designs of God this unrighteous government policy was introduced to test the faithfulness of those who claimed Christ as their "all in all." I am happy to say that a great many churches and Christian organizations saw this as an opportunity to sever their ties and dependency on the powers of the secular state. I know of some that used this providential opportunity to reassess the foundation upon which their organization developed, asking themselves, "Do we really have faith at all?"

However, other organizations acquiesced to the government requirement. In direct contrast to the woman who gave up her family and friends for Christ, these organizations betrayed their confidence in His sufficiency. It is God's Providence, displayed in situations we face, that opens our eyes to whether we have ever trusted in Christ in the first place.

Faith is trust. It is confidence in God. That confidence has an objective basis. And for this faith we would gladly disabuse ourselves of all other things so that we might gain Christ. In his Providence, God orders the events in our lives to allow us to see if we have faith or not.

CHAPTER 15

Providence Says, "Be Content"

I don't believe even half of what is said by motivational speakers. In my younger years there was a popular preacher who was really a motivational speaker. He used to say, "Tough times never last, but tough people do." Many people loved it when he said that. He told people that, no matter the obstacles, anyone with the right attitude could prevail. "Your problems," he said, "are not tougher than you are." He said all you had to do was take on your problems one step at a time. "Inch by inch, everything's a cinch," he told his followers. "When life gives you lemons, make lemonade."

Of course, the reason for his popularity was because all his words seemed so empowering. But while some of it was true, a great deal more was false. Luke 12 records Jesus's parable of the rich fool. The man had land that was extremely fertile, so he decided to build bigger barns and achieve a luxurious life off his productive land. But God called this man a fool. He was planning on something he did not have. He was planning on a future. God required his soul of him the very night he was making his plans. Only God decides how long tough times or tough people last. We plan but God decides. Tough people, it turns out, never last. Psalm 102:11 illustrates the fragility of life: "My days are like an evening shadow; I wither away like grass."

So do David's words in Psalm 103:15–16: "As for man, his days are like grass; he flourishes like a flower of the field; for the wind passes over it, and it is gone, and its place knows it no more."

Psalm 90:4–6 records the thoughts of Moses:

> For a thousand years in your sight are but as yesterday
> when it is past,
> or as a watch in the night.
> You sweep them [that is, people] away as with a flood;
> they are like a dream, like grass that is renewed in the
> morning:
> in the morning it flourishes and is renewed;
> in the evening it fades and withers.

Several verses later, in Verse 9, Moses adds: "For all our days pass away under your wrath; we bring our years to an end like a sigh."

Finishing well

Books have been written about "finishing well." It is an attractive thought. Who wouldn't love to end their lives on a high note? To those who write wisely about these things, the emphasis is on living in faithfulness to Christ to the end of our lives. This is a good thought. We should all be encouraged by Paul's words in 2 Timothy 4:7: "I have fought the good fight, I have finished the race, I have kept the faith."

Every Christian at the end of their lives should want to say the same thing. We should want to end on a note of triumph and look back with satisfaction at a life well lived in Christ.

A man in his senior years once gave me an interesting thought about aging. He said the temptations he faced as a young man are different than the temptations he faces now. "But," he said, "the temptations at my age are as great a struggle as the ones I faced when young. The battle to remain faithful to the Lord continues to be a fight until we draw our last breath."

While we pray for grace to remain faithful to the end, many of us will finish with a whimper. It may be true that Moses died at 120 years of age, with eyes undimmed and vigour unabated, but it will not be so with many faithful servants of Jesus. Our eyesight and hearing may fail. We may find it difficult to move around. Some of us will develop Alzheimer's or get cancer. We may wind up living in a care home, relying on others to care for us. Influence we may have had when we were at the place of vigour will have gone. Many faithful saints will have remained faithful, but will pass from this world with a gradual waning of life and forgotten in this world. What are we to make of them? Did they finish well?

I love to recount the turn of events and the end-of-life stories of some of the heroes of the faith. Athanasius of Alexandra, the man who safeguarded the doctrine of the Trinity and kept the Church from abandoning the true God, was banished from the empire. John Chrysostom, archbishop of Constantinople, was kicked out of his pulpit and Roman soldiers walked him at such a pace that they marched him to death. Katherine, the wife of Martin Luther, was warned by her husband that marrying him would not be a good deal for her. After his death she lived a life of poverty. English Baptist preacher Charles Haddon Spurgeon was so maligned, even by his own brother, that his widow claimed the stress led to his early death. Jonathan Edwards was kicked out of his pulpit. The list goes on and on.

Are you surprised? Why should you be? Our Lord was crucified on a Roman cross. So much for ending strong, if by that we mean with people speaking well of us, or that we are vigorous to the end. If it is the will of God that you die in vigour, be grateful.

I often think of the difference between my father's and my mother's death. My father was intellectually clear until he passed. He spoke of his hope in Christ and encouraged his children on. In the estimation of many, he died well. My mother had Alzheimer's for years and couldn't speak or recognize anyone. Finally she stopped eating. When we asked if we should tube-feed her, the doctor said it would probably fill her lungs with fluid, leading her to drown. We refused any emergency measures for her and said the Lord's will would be done. Eventually she passed away, not recognizing her family around her and in a complete fog of confusion.

Tough or weak, none of us last. We are like grass. All the things we do, the earthly identities we hold dear—worker, husband, wife, mother, father—are left behind at some point. Life will, as the motivational speaker/pastor said, give you lemons, but at the end of your life you won't be able to make lemonade out of everything. Don't believe those who tell half-truths. It will leave you shocked and disillusioned in the end.

Have I depressed you enough? I hope you are paying attention! We are not the tough lords of our own future, we are the grass of the field. And as for those bravado obituaries in which it is common to read that a certain loved one will never be forgotten, understand this also to be deceit. The great majority of those who die every day will be forgotten in this world. It may be true that their loved ones are determined to keep their memory alive, but their loved ones will also be forgotten.

This world will disappoint you

The point of this realistic talk about the end of our lives is this: if your hope is rooted in this world rather than the one to come, there is no good ending. The "possibility preachers" and the motivational speakers are attractive because they offer a version of joy many would dearly love to have. But the truth is that most of us will not catch the attention of the world; instead, we will live with some successes and failures, and when we die this world will remember us no more. That is the truth. As Solomon said in Ecclesiastes 1:2, "Vanity of vanities, says the Preacher, vanity of vanities! All is vanity"

I find harsh realism far more refreshing than sugar-coated lies. Lies don't set us free. But the truth can.

Is there reason to be content?

Should any sane and thoughtful person have reason to be content? For those who embrace the doctrine of Providence, the answer is a resounding yes! However, those who look for earthly contentment—and the gullible ones who listen to motivational speakers—will not find contentment. Perhaps they will for a time, but the reality of the course of every life will lead them to despair. I often wonder how those without faith do not sink into despondency and anguish.

Think about the classic midlife crisis. Perhaps a man or woman gets to be about forty-five years of age and realizes that their life is half over, given average life expectancies. Grief and panic ensue as they think, *It's half over! I have accomplished so little. I have not yet fulfilled my destiny! What if my accomplishments in the second half don't match my expectations? Precious time is ticking away. How much time might I reasonably expect?*

In desperation, some try to recapture their youth. They undergo surgery to remove wrinkles from their faces, they dress as if they were younger, some divorce their spouses and try to recapture the carefree days of youth. Solomon would say that this is vanity. I say it's delusional. Ask an eighteen-year-old if that forty-five-year-old man or woman looks young and they will quickly tell you they do not. These panicking people do not fool the young, they fool themselves.

I love to tell sixty-year-olds that they are not middle-aged. Ice hockey has three periods that make up a full game. A sixty-year-old is definitely in the last period of the game. Two periods have been spent, and by now they should know that a period passes at great speed. Furthermore, the game of life can always end early.

The next moment of panic comes along with the senior years of life. Some people continue to work in these years, and there's nothing wrong with that if it is enjoyable and fulfilling, or if they need the money. But if they continue to work because they fear giving up on the dream that there is still something great they might yet accomplish, that is delusional. There comes a moment when we realize that no more great accomplishments lie ahead. Whatever difference we made, or thought we made, now lies behind us, and a great many people must face the fact that they made a far smaller impact than they expected. If they were Christians, perhaps they were going to win the world for Christ, or change the church for the better, or teach the next generation not to make the same mistakes they did. But now, what has been done is done. The striving is over.

Are you depressed yet? I hope you are. I wish to divest you of all dreams that the fulfilment you seek will happen in *this* life. You should come to believe that the best you can do in this life is to be faithful to that which our Lord calls you to do. If you do that with all your might, you have lived well. Accomplishments in this life only matter if they reflect obedience to the one who created you. The desire to leave a mark in this world is really a form of idolatry. It is an attempt to overcome our own finitude. It is an attempt to be eternal through our own genius and effort. It is the vanity of which Solomon speaks.

Some do make a lasting impact

Some people do, indeed, make a lasting impact on this world. Whether for good or bad, their names are remembered. Think for a moment of the lasting impact of a craftsman in Germany named Johannes Gutenberg. Think of how the world was changed with the invention of his printing press. Or think of Alexander Fleming, whose discovery of penicillin saved countless lives. The list of people and events that have bettered humanity are many. Furthermore, humanity has remembered some of these visionary, farsighted men and women, such as William Wilberforce, who campaigned to end slavery in England. His unwillingness to give up under a withering barrage of criticism is inspiring.

But better than all the difference-makers are the men and women who bring the glorious Gospel of Jesus Christ to people and lands who have never heard of Him. My friend—the best man at my wedding—and his wife have given their lives to a village in Central America, bringing literacy and Gospel witness there, starting a Christian school and planting a church. Their efforts raised a generation of children out of poverty, and now some of the graduates of their school have returned to serve and lift the next generation in the villiage, with the skills they now possess. I recently spoke with them, and they told me they expect to die in that village where they have served. They may not have changed the world, but they did change one village in it. Many in the Kingdom of Heaven will point to them as the catalyst that brought them to the saving news of Jesus. May God raise up many more like them!

We should rejoice that many people have lived lives that glorify God in this way, and we should celebrate their achievements. We should also celebrate the great heroes of our faith, but sadly many Christians can't name a single noteworthy Christian since the New Testament was completed. Because of that, many don't dream of the things that might be accomplished in faith and obedience to Christ.

But as much as we should take inspiration from those whose lives have made a difference, we do badly if we think that we should aspire to greatness. Greatness should not be the goal; do not seek to leave a name that outlasts its time. Be content to serve the Lord Christ according to the gifts He has assigned to you. Respond to the promptings of the Holy Spirit. Do faithfully that which your hand finds to do. Worry little if your footprint is large or small.

How to be content with your life

We do well to remember 1 Corinthians 7:17: "Only let each person lead the life that the Lord has assigned to him, and to which God has called him."

What does that mean? Regardless of the situation in which you find yourself, find your assignment from God and live faithfully within it. Be content with your assignment. Further, 1 Corinthians 4:7 asks, "What do you have that you did not receive?"

The things we have received from God include the talents we have and the life situation we were born into. It also includes the time in which we live and the opportunities available to us. All these things are given by God.

Let's agree that some of the people who made a great difference in the world had the right confluence of factors to help them along, including natural talent and access to education, the levers of political power, technology and the health and strength to sustain them in life. If these things were not present they would never have been able to accomplish the things they did. The doctrine of Providence reminds us that these things are not random, but planned by the ever-wise hand of God.

Paul encourages believers to lead the life the Lord has assigned them. It is important that we don't fight God's providential arrangements. If God gave you opportunities to be a rocket scientist, then pursue it with all your might. But if you live in a small village in El Salvador and have little access to the advantages of those who live in the industrialized world, you can still live for the glory of God. Consider 1 Corinthians 7:21: "Were you a bondservant when called? Do not be concerned about it." But if you can gain your freedom, avail yourself of the opportunity.

In short, you might be able to gain your freedom. But you might not.

Why Providence leads to contentment

I have said a great deal about false and true optimism. I want to dash all hope that this life and this world is a theatre for our greatness. I think the counsel that God gave Jeremiah ought to be standard Christian counsel. Jeremiah 45:5 records God speaking to the prophet: "And do you seek great things for yourself? Seek them not, for behold, I am bringing disaster upon all flesh, declares the Lord."

In short, God wanted Jeremiah to avoid a high position. Jerusalem was going to fall to the Babylonian army, and if Jeremiah was in an influential office he would become a target for the invading Babylonians. The message is, "Now is not the time for seeking greatness."

This is a valuable lesson. Our times determine our opportunities, and these times are in God's hands, not ours. In His wise Providence, God will ordain and sustain that which is for His glory and the eternal good of His people.

For this reason we should not fret if our opportunities to make an impact are less than those afforded to others. If our goal in life is to seek great things for ourselves, we are offside. God, in His wise and providential plans, determines what we accomplish. All those verses about being like grass, like a brief vapour, should be taken to heart. Most of us end this life not in a blaze of glory, but in a small way. But we need not fear, for God has determined both our beginning and our ending.

How can we live life with undying optimism? Where can such a life be found?

1 Corinthians 15 details the resurrection of the dead and tells how our earthly bodies will one day be transformed like Christ's glorious body. The very last verse in that chapter says, "Therefore, my beloved brothers, be steadfast, immovable, always abounding in the work of the Lord, knowing that in the Lord your labour is not in vain."

Notice the passage doesn't say, "Therefore, since you have learned about the resurrection, begin to speculate when that might happen and lose interest in the world of here and now." Instead, 1 Corinthians 15:58 says that what Christians do for the kingdom of God will bring results that last forever. What we do in this world for the future Kingdom will never be forgotten.

Years ago I spent some time with a man who was involved in church planting, both in Germany and Russia. He told me that his life had turned out quite differently from what he had projected. He was planning a career in the automotive industry. He thought he would be one of those elite engineers who design new cars. That was not to be. Instead, he became a missionary. One day when I was with him, we were travelling from one location in Germany to another, following a certain car. He was commenting on the design of the rear taillight. He told me, "I almost spent my entire life investing in the design of taillights. When my life was through, I would have said, 'I managed to exert a powerful influence on how taillights look and function on vehicles.' You could have looked at the rear of a car and thought of me. Instead, I will have influenced the eternity of men and women."

Indeed! An investment in taillights, or in eternity. When a million years have come and gone, not one of those taillights will even remotely matter.

Whatever you do in the work of the Lord is not in vain, though it may be discounted now. Jesus said in Luke 16:15, "What is exalted among men is an abomination in the sight of God."

You must figure out where to make your investment. If you were to become a president or prime minister in this world, I promise you that in a million years not one person will remember your name. But if you invest in a Sunday school class and influence one child to trust eternally in Jesus, your work in the Lord will never be forgotten.

Colossians 3:23-24 says, "Whatever you do, work heartily, as for the Lord and not for men, knowing that from the Lord you will receive the inheritance as your reward. You are serving the Lord Christ."

And 1 Peter 1:18 says, "That you were ransomed from the futile ways inherited from your forefathers."

Let's tie all this together with the doctrine of God's daily Providence in our lives. When we are not content and we complain about the way our lives are turning out, we cast aspersions on the wise and benevolent Providence of God. God has ordained your ways. God made you in a way that pleases Him. Perhaps you are not the best-looking person in the world. Perhaps others have a greater intellect than yours. Perhaps the opportunities that come to you are not as great as those that come to others. What should you do? You should take delight in the Providence of God. Pray earnestly for a heart that delights in the fact that God has designed you exactly as you are for His divine reasons.

Spend your life rejoicing in God's plan for you. Don't spend your life wanting to be someone else. Serve the Lord with all your heart. Know that whenever you live by faith in obedience to His commands, your life is not in vain. Rejoice in the opportunities God has given you.

All of this leads to deep, abiding satisfaction. As a Christian, I am keenly aware of two things. First, God is preparing me today to maximize my eternal joy, and that even the sorrows I face are for that end. Second, my best days lie ahead of me. Yes, I know a coffin and a grave lie before me if Christ delays his coming, but I will not fear, for even the death God has reserved for me is serving His glory and my long-term good. The doctrine of Providence fills me with contentment and joy. I rejoice in Romans 8:28:

> And we know that for those who love God all things work together for good, for those who are called according to His purpose.

EPILOGUE

Richard and Nancy Harrison sat down to take stock of the last year. It had unfortunately been filled with disappointments. As they discussed the events of the last twelve months, they came up with the phrase "an unfortunately memorable year." How they hoped the coming new year would offer them a reprieve.

Until the misfortunes that had been thrust upon them during last year, they had thought of their lives as wonderful. They had a good marriage. They each had respectable, well-compensated employment. Their children were grown and married to good Christian spouses and were active in the church and doing well.

And then everything changed. Richard was unjustly fired from his job at the age of fifty-nine, an age where it is difficult to find another job. Their daughter told them her marriage was unstable and that her husband was verbally and physically abusive. She said the children were afraid of him and that he'd had multiple sexual affairs. As if this wasn't bad enough, their son was badly injured in a motor vehicle accident. With proper care, in several years he could be rehabilitated; in the meantime he was unable to work. It was heartbreaking.

It was too much for Richard. Always active in prayer and ministry, he suddenly found himself unable to pray. He withdrew from friends and his easy smile disappeared. Weariness and pain were reflected on his face, as if a helplessness had gripped his spirit. He couldn't sleep, and while he still went to church, he sat at the back and hurried out the door when it was done. Further, Richard thought that Nancy didn't understand how painful his unjust firing had been, and so he withdrew from her as well.

At one time Richard was one of the most respected men in his profession, now he knew people were saying things like, "He must have really screwed up!" and "I guess we overestimated him."

Meanwhile, Nancy didn't know how to respond to her increasingly withdrawn husband. She felt unable to reach him, and their once-model marriage, although not in danger of divorce, was becoming two solitudes living together.

But Richard had one truth his heart would not abandon. Somehow he seized on Genesis 50:20 and started repeating it to himself multiple times each day. He couldn't let it go: "You intended it to harm me, but God intended it for good."

Often, as he repeated the verse he found it difficult to believe. He readily grasped the first part of the verse: "You intended it to harm me." Those who'd falsely maligned him, resulting in the loss of his position, surely intended to harm him. Their slanderous assassination of his character had done its work, while these men had acted as if they were his friends. By the time he knew what was going on, the damage had been done.

Yes, thought Richard, *I believe the first part of this verse. They intended it to harm me. No matter how they justified their behaviour, such slander was horribly destructive. They were merciless, false and unconcerned with the damage they did to me.*

He would have preferred they had murdered him, and to make matters worse the men who had done these things were active churchgoers! Oh, how painful it all was. They had intended harm. They had intended to do evil.

But Richard also repeated the latter half of the verse. God intended it for good. After all, God sustained all things, and so without God's sustaining hand these men would have been unable to do what they did. Did God will that these men treat him this way? Was God the reason these men had done the things they did?

If this was so (and Richard believed it was), there were only two options open to him.

He could do what Job's wife counselled her husband to do: "Curse God and die." When Richard thought about it, he remembered some in his church who had done exactly that. They had dropped out of church. They had gradually become godless. Their prayer lives had ceased. They got used to living without God.

But the other option was the one Richard clung to: God intended it for good. How could that be true? How could the devastation in his job and in his family ever turn out for good? If Richard were honest, his repetition of the words "he intended it for good" had been reduced to a rote incantation. He wasn't sure he believed it. But somewhere inside of his soul he knew he must never forget to repeat the words. "He intended it for good. He intended it for good. He intended it for good."

Repeating the words didn't lesson his pain, change the situation or give him instant hope; however, it gave Richard something more precious: it prevented him from sliding into a spiritual abyss. He realized that if those words were not true it reduced all of life to random chance, a flip of the coin. Without those words he would curse God and die or embrace meaninglessness, which would also lead to death. And so Richard continued repeating the words.

Richard and Nancy step into God's future

Several things happened that caused the darkened clouds to lighten. Out of the blue, Richard received a phone call from a company on the brink of failure that desperately needed someone with Richard's skills. A key employee had retired—would Richard like the job?

With no other options Richard said yes, though the pay was less and the future of the company doubtful. *Perhaps this new employment will last only a year,* he thought, *but at least it will take me one year closer to retirement.*

He started the job with a certain level of uncertainty, but then something surprising happened. Instead of failure, the company began to turn around. Amazingly, Richard's skills were key to this and he had come to this position at just the right time. Growth ensued and the company moved from success to success. Richard found he was enjoying himself, and continued working well past the usual age of retirement.

The new job offered him opportunities he would never have had in his old position, and he enjoyed it very much. As he reflected on it, some of the opportunities were more than he could have dreamt of. He found himself with openings he would never have enjoyed had he stayed with the old company.

The situation with his children's struggles also changed, but at a slower pace. There were no quick turnarounds, just slow and steady slogging, but the steps were forward and not back.

However, one thing didn't change: there was a wound in Richard that just wouldn't heal. It did not become bitterness, but it remained open and raw. The wound was shock at how easily his colleagues had struck out and hurt him. He never quite got over the feeling of betrayal. And as to how God would use that for good, it remained a mystery. But Richard also learned from this. How often had he wounded others, he wondered. A greater care for the lives of others began to take shape in his heart.

But as time went on and the most difficult year of his life slowly faded into his past, a growing and abiding conviction that the year was intended for good started to take hold, and he realized that he no longer had to force himself to believe that God had intended the events of that year for good. He believed it with intensity and certainty, though he couldn't explain how. His level of trust in the plans of God had entered his heart with a resolve he had never known before.

There was one more thing that happened to Richard. During a Good Friday service, as the sufferings of Jesus were recounted, Richard found himself weeping uncontrollably during the recounting of the slander that had been levelled at Jesus. The high priests wanted false witnesses and they had arisen, twisting the truth so that Jesus was made to appear like a political revolutionary. They said that Jesus had intended to destroy the temple and begin a war with Rome. Richard had heard the story before, but on this occasion he had eyes to see and a heart to feel the slander. The betrayal of Judas struck him as never before.

During that service, Richard bowed his head and began to pour out his soul to God. For the first time since his troubles began, he thanked God for the slander he had undergone. He had come to realize that if he had not experienced it, he never would have understood the suffering of Jesus, nor would he have understood the depth of his Saviour's love for him.

Why Providence changes everything

The Providence of God is the sustaining principle for a lifetime of faith. Richard and Nancy are fictitious people, but they are also a compilation of some people I have met and who have experienced situations like this.

What a tragedy it is when God's Providence is neither known nor believed. How do we find our way through pain, disappointment, tragedy and reversal of fortune? What solace will we find when men and women speak words to betray and destroy us? Knowing that the loving hand of our faithful, saving God sustains all things is the assurance we need that nothing, not even a devastating year, can separate us from the love of Christ. Hardship will only throw us more resolutely onto Him. Danger will make us courageous. Nakedness will make us rely on His provision. Threats will focus our hearts on His protection.

The doctrine of Providence forces us to think deeply on the dealings of God in every area of our lives. If we let it, it will make excellent theologians of us. It will also be the key to living well. It will give us the tools to be faithful to Christ to the end, make us thankful in all things and help us see God—not on occasion, but in all things.

To Him be the glory.